Revolutionary Boston, Lexington, and Concord

The Shots Heard Round the World!

Modern Myths and Revolutionary Realities
★ *1775 to Today* ★

By *Joseph L. Andrews, Jr., M.D.*
Author, Editor and Photographer
and Contributors

Concord Guides Press

Concord, Massachusetts
U.S.A.

★ ★ ★ ★

First Edition, Published as a Paperback, on April 19, 1998 as:
Revolutionary Lexington and Concord:
The Shot(s) Heard Round The World!
Printed by Minute Man Press, Concord, Massachusetts, U.S.A.
ISBN Number: 0-9664112-0-X
Library of Congress Catalog Number: 98-175-942

This Revised, Augmented **Second Edition**, Published on April 19, 1999 as:
Revolutionary Boston, Lexington and Concord:
The Shots Heard Round The World!
Printed by Intercity Press, Rockland, Massachusetts, U.S.A.
Print Broker: Jim Coveno, Data Associates, Weston and Waltham, Massachusetts
Graphic Designer: Valerie Bessette
ISBN Number: 0-9664112-1-8
Library of Congress Catalog Number: pending

Major parts of the text first appeared as an article, *Lexington & Concord: 1775/1997*, by Joseph L. Andrews, Jr., M.D. in the Spring, 1997 *S.A.R. Magazine*, Winston C. Williams, Editor, published by the National Society of the Sons of the American Revolution (S.A.R.), 1000 South Fourth Street, Louisville, Kentucky 40203, and are reprinted here with their kind permission.

Concord Guides & Press is a member of the Concord Chamber of Commerce, Concord, MA. and the Greater Merrimack Valley Convention and Visitors Bureau, Lowell, MA

★ ★ ★ ★

For Jennifer, Sara & Joe

For All The Paxtons, Kotzens and Eldridges

In Loving Memory Of:

★

My Parents
Katherine New Andrews
Joseph Lyon Andrews

★

My Wife
Margareta Langert Andrews

★

My Sister
Ann Andrews Paxton

★

My Uncle
Sidney New, Jr.

★ ★ ★ ★

★ ★ ★ ★

Paul Revere in Boston, 1768. Portrait by John Singleton Copley.

Front Cover Painting: Along the Battle Road, April 19, 1775. The front cover shows the large mural displayed at the Minute Man Visitors' Center on the Battle Road (now Route 2 A near the Lexington/Lincoln line). It was painted by Chicago artist John Rush for the Minute Man National Historical Park of the National Park Service. It depicts combat between the British Redcoats, retreating from Concord to Boston along the Battle Road in the so-called "running skirmish" between the British Redcoats and the colonial militia and Minutemen from many neighboring towns, who pursued them. The action portrayed here took place at about 1:30 P.M. near Nelson Road, just west of the Visitors' Center. *(Courtesy of Minute Man National Historical Park, National Park Service.)*

★ ★ ★ ★

Table of Contents

Detail of **The Engagement at the North Bridge** in Concord by Ralph Earle/ Amos Doolittle (1775) depicts the clash at about 9:30 A.M. on April 19, 1775 between British Regulars and the Colonial militia and Minutemen, who have just descended from the hill on the north bank of the river. Two Americans and three Redcoats were killed during the brief but deadly encounter, which lasted no more than two minutes.

★ ★ ★ ★

★ ★ ★ ★

*Chapters and photographs which are not specifically attributed in this book
were created by the author, Joseph L. Andrews, Jr., M.D.*

★ ★ ★ ★

Preface to the Second Edition

After the First Edition of this book was published in 1998, many people asked me why I wrote a book about the beginning of the American Revolution in the Boston and Lexington and Concord areas. The story of why I wrote this book in the first place is worth telling.

When I moved to Concord, MA in 1995, I took courses at Concord's Adult Education program, read, attended lectures and participated in community organizations to learn more about Concord's extraordinary historic, literary and natural heritage. After passing an extensive exam on these subjects, I became a Licensed Concord Guide. Then I volunteered as a guide at the Concord Visitors'

The Old Manse (c. 1770), on Monument Street in Concord overlooks the Concord River and the North Bridge. Originally home to minister Rev. William Emerson, it is where his grandson Ralph Waldo Emerson wrote his most famous essays and for several years served as the honeymoon house for author Nathaniel Hawthorne and his bride. As an historic house, it is a gem to visit, since it still houses many of its original furnishings. A modern Minuteman and Redcoat confer...peacefully.

★ PREFACE ★

Samuel Adams in Boston, about 1772. Portrait in oils by John Singleton Copley.

Information Booth and later began to personally guide visitors from around the world as well as area residents, as part of Concord Guides Walking Tours, which I had started with the help of other Concord guides.

I was frequently asked by visitors, residents and students alike if there was a good **introductory history/ guide book** about the area, which was **accurate, readable, succinct** and **affordable**. My answer was that, although there were many brochures and also academic tomes about various aspects of the area, I knew of **no comprehensive, coordinated introductory guide** with all the features that they desired.

So, with the audacity and optimism, that only a naïve newcomer can muster, I decided to combine my experience as a free-lance writer with my curiosity as a history buff to write an introduction to the Boston/ Lexington/ Concord area's rich Revolutionary **history,** with an accompanying guide to its abundant historical **sites**.

Since I felt strongly that it was very important to share with others the inspiring, fascinating stories of American's early struggles to achieve independence and freedom, both the tragedies and the triumphs, I decided to publish the book myself. The rest, as they say, is history. The details of what it takes to self-publish a book for the first time could make for an interesting book itself. But here is not the place to recount the pitfalls and pleasures of self-publishing.

Suffice it to say that I made a lot of mistakes. But in so doing I learned a lot. With the help of Jim Steinmann of Minute Man Press in West Concord, who met my unreasonable requests with hard work and a smile, we printed the book by my (self-imposed) Patriots' Day deadline with only hours to spare. Jim persuaded me to seek the support of Sponsors, to help pay his bills and to keep the price of the book as low as possible to appeal to a large audience.

Reactions to the First Edition were generally positive and we completely sold out the First Edition in several months. However, a few critics complained about what our short (64 page) book did *not* have. Why all the hype about Lexington and Concord's roles in the Revolution? How about Arlington? Acton? Cambridge?

★ PREFACE ★

More details about Boston? Where were the women? Blacks? Native Americans?

Hence, this **Second Edition** was launched. Here we have more than doubled the narrative content and have added chapters written by contributing authors, about five additional towns and their roles in the events of April 18 and 19, 1775. We have also added chapters about the roles of diverse groups at the start of the Revolution.

This book is organized as two parallel texts, related to each other and closely coordinated. A narrative **history** of the momentous events which occurred around Boston at the beginning of the Revolution, particularly in 1775 and 1776, in each of nine different towns in the Boston area is fol-

John Hancock in Boston, 1765. Portrait by John Singleton Copley.

lowed in each chapter by descriptions of the most important **Revolutionary sites** for a visitor to see in each town.

The temporal and geographic links between the *events* and the *sites* are made with the aid of maps and timelines. For example, the Alarm Map, depicts *where* and *when* the alarm was spread by riders from Boston westward to Cambridge, Arlington, Lexington, Lincoln, Concord, Acton, Bedford and Sudbury— this sequence of towns also being how the chapters are organized. The Hour by Hour Chronicle details the time sequence of these events in the different towns. "Sources" at the end of each chapter will permit each reader to explore, in more depth, topics that intrigue him.

Please use this book as either a pocket reference to enhance your enjoyment and historical understanding when you visit the Boston area, or for later study of topics of interest, or simply to read for pleasure and edification. But, by all means, I hope that you do use it and enjoy it!

Modern day re-enactors costumed as British Redcoats.

★ INTRODUCTION ★

Modern Myths and Revolutionary Realities

"The British are coming!" shouted Paul Revere.

"If they mean to have a war, let it begin here!" asserted Captain John Parker at Lexington Green.

"Don't fire till you see the whites of their eyes!" yelled Colonel Prescott at Bunker Hill.

When asked about the American Revolution, many Americans, who have only hazy memories of their school history courses, remember only a few "historic" quotes like these. Yet, many people are shocked to learn that the historical accuracy of all these three "quotes" is questionable because: A) There are no authenticated contemporary accounts verifying that these words were actually spoken by these men, and, B) in the historical context in which these phrases were uttered, it is unlikely that these men would have expressed these thoughts or used these words. In other words, these statements, as dramatic as they are, are more modern **myths** than Revolutionary realities.

Readers will find the questions about the authenticity of these three "quotes" and about many other widely accepted "facts" about the American Revolution discussed more thoroughly in the chapters of this book. The reader will also gain more insight into the controversy surrounding of the following widely accepted myths about the Revolution:

Myth: The American Revolution was really not as important as other wars, like the Civil War. **Reality:** Colonists, who originally thought of themselves as "British Americans," risked their lives in the fight to guarantee *human rights* which after independence became guaranteed in the Constitution and Bill of Rights.

Myth: Colonial Patriots consisted exclusively of white, Protestant males of British descent. **Reality:** American Patriots included in their ranks many diverse people, as detailed in chapters on women, blacks and Native Americans.

Myth: All American colonists supported the Revolutionary effort. **Reality:** Only about one-third of Americans were Patriots, one-third were Tories, loyal to the King, and the other third were neutral or indifferent.

Myth: Most of the early action took place in Boston. **Reality:** As is described in many chapters in this book, many other towns and other states were involved in the early days of the Revolution from Cambridge to Concord.

Myth: We have nothing new to learn about the Revolution today. **Reality:** There are still many unresolved controversies, as can be seen by the discussions in this book.

This book will help the reader re-examine his previous notions about the Revolution (many **myths**) and replace them with more accurate knowledge (Revolutionary **realities**)!

★ PRELUDE TO THE AMERICAN REVOLUTION ★
A CHRONOLOGY: 1756-1776

1756-1763 **French and Indian (Seven Years') War** is a conflict between England and France over land and furs. England feels it must raise funds to pay for the cost of this war.

1760 **George III** becomes King of England. **Writs of Assistance** grant search warrants to the Boston Royal Customs Officer.

1761 James Otis argues against Writs.

1763 **Treaty of Paris** ends the War. **Faneuil Hall** in Boston is dedicated to the "Cause of Liberty" by Otis.

1764 **Sugar Act** raises revenues for the King for defense.

1765 **Stamp Act** requires tax stamps for newspapers, licenses and deeds. Mobs riot in Boston, demolish stamp office, hang effigy of Stamp Officer from the "Liberty Tree" elm. Stamp Act Congress in New York sends protests to the King, Lords and Commons for "subverting the rights and liberties of the colonies."

1766 **Stamp Act repealed** following British merchants' losses from Americas **non-importation agreements**. Sons of Liberty lead celebrations in Boston.

1767 **Townshend Acts** passed by Parliament, legalize Writs of Assistance and impose import duties on tea, lead, glass, and paper.

1768 Samuel Adams encourages **Circular Letters** to other colonies, protesting new taxes. Boston mob attacks Customs Commissioner. General Thomas Gage arrives in Boston to take personal command of augmented British troops.

1769 **Boston Town Meeting** urges **boycott** of British-made goods.

1770 March 5: "**Boston Massacre**". Harassed British soldiers fire into crowd, kill five, injure six. Six British soldiers, defended by Josiah Quincy and John Adams, are found not guilty; two, declared guilty of manslaughter, are branded.

1771 Thomas Hutchinson is appointed the **Royal Governor**, with his salary to be paid by the Crown from Colonial revenues, which dismays Patriots.

1772 **Committees of Correspondence**, led by James Otis, Samuel Adams and Dr. Joseph Warren of Boston, protest Governor Hutchinson's "depotism" and affirm "rights of the colonists."

1773 **Tea Act** passed by Parliament, favors British East India Company tea sales.

Dec. 16: **Boston Tea Party**: Colonists disguised as "Indians" empty 342 chests of tea into the Boston Harbor in protest of the Tea Act.

1774

"**Intolerable Acts**": These retaliatory coercive acts are passed by Parliament; Port of Boston is closed; Charter of Massachusetts. Bay Colony is annulled; public town meetings—the glory of New England's heritage—are now to be held only by permission of the Governor. British troops must now be quartered in private homes.

May 13: Appointed by George III, **General Thomas Gage** arrives in Boston to take over Governorship, as well as to command all British troops in Massachusetts.

May 14: Boston Town Meeting proposes to other colonies to **ban all imports from and exports to Great Britain.**

September 1: General Gage sends two companies of soldiers to seize powder in an arsenal in Charlestown. (The **powder house** site is in today's Somerville.)

September: **Massachusetts General Court** (legislature) sends five delegates to the **Continental Congress** in Philadelphia, to meet with delegates from the 13 Colonies.

Dedham Resolves declare "no obedience" to "wicked" Parliament's acts, which "enslave America." Resolves adopted by Continental Congress on September 17.

October: **Gen. Gage cancels the General Court** (Massachusetts legislature) scheduled for Salem. Delegates gather in **Concord** at the First Parish Church to form the **First Provincial Congress**, with John Hancock as President. They form an executive Committee of Safety, which creates a company of "**militia Minutemen** to hold themselves in readiness at a minute's warning, compleat in arms and ammunition, good and sufficient firelock, thirty rounds of powder and ball, pouch and knapsack."

October: The Congress assigns Col. James Barret of Concord to collect and store supplies for a Patriots' army of up to 15,000 men. **Concord is chosen to hide the military supplies,** because of its central location and its "safe" distance from British troops, quartered in Boston.

1775

Feb. 1: **Second Provincial Congress** in Cambridge urges "minute men" to drill and arm.

Feb. 9: Parliament declares Massachusetts to be in a **state of rebellion.**

Feb. 26: Gen. Gage sends troops to **Salem** to seize military stores; they find none.

March: Provincial Patriot leaders station guards in Concord and place **couriers** along the route to Concord to **alarm** the countryside, should British troops march from Boston to Concord to seize military supplies.

April 18-19: **Battles of Lexington and Concord** followed by the **"running skirmish,"** during which British soldiers retreat eastward back to Boston along the Battle Road, pursued by American militia and Minutemen from over thirty towns. *(See separate Chronology: April 18-19, 1775.)*

April 19: **Siege of Boston begins**. The British fleet blockades Boston Harbor. American soldiers surround Boston.

April 23: Provincial Congress authorizes an **American Army** of 13,000 men.

May 24: John Hancock is elected President of **Second Continental Congress** in Philadelphia.

May 25: **British Generals** Howe, Burgoyne and Clinton arrive in Boston.

June 12: General Gage proclaims **martial law** in Boston.

June 17: British troops attack and rout America's forces at **Breed's Hill** in Charlestown and then **Bunker Hill**. Americans regroup in Cambridge.

July 3: **George Washington arrives in Cambridge** to command the newly formed **Continental Army**.

1776

March 4-5: Americans fortify **Dorchester Heights**, overlooking Boston from the south. American cannons are now within firing range of British ships below in Boston Harbor.

March 17: **Evacuation Day**. British troops, government officials and Loyalists **sail out of Boston Harbor**, never to return.

July 4: **Declaration of Independence** is adopted in Philadelphia by the Continental Congress. ¬J.L.A

Source: Fiore, Jordan, Massachusetts in Ferment: The Coming of the American Revolution, A Chronological Survey, 1760-1775, Massachusetts Bicentennial Commission, 1971.

★ ★ ★ ★

Boston and Bunker Hill: From Royalty to Rebellion

lthough modern skyscrapers tower above the center of today's Boston, the city is unique in America in that it still retains a great many original distinctive landmarks from its earliest history. Fortuitously and often against great odds, these irreplaceable national treasures have been preserved and survive today, unlike many other large American cities, where land-mark structures often encounter more wrecking balls than visitors. Traditional Boston neighborhoods, closely associated with America's past, co-exist with near-by modern bustling Boston.

Bostonians–and visitors to Boston—don't just read about American history, they *live* it. They still worship in Colonial churches, built when George III was not only King of England, but of Boston as well. Daily they walk past Boston's Revolutionary era buildings on worn brick sidewalks and narrow cobblestoned streets and study at its many venerable world- renowned universities. In Boston, history is not dead. It is all around you, always helping to inform and to inspire you.

A walk around Boston will transport the visitor past structures and sites, span-ning over three and a half centuries of American history. Dating back to early settlement by English Puritans in the **1600's** are the **Boston Common** (1622), the

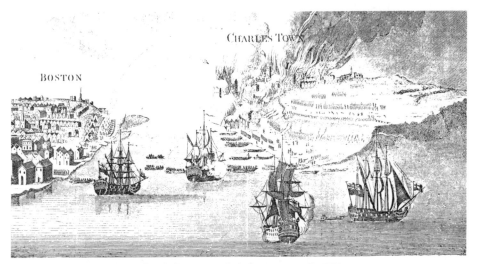

View of the Attack on Bunker's Hill with the Burning of Charlestown, June 17, 1775.

The Boston Tea Party Ship is where in 1773 irate Colonists, disguised as Indians, threw 342 chests of tea—about 60 tons of tea leaves—into the Boston Harbor to protest the Tea Tax. Pictured here is Beaver II, a replica of one of the three ships involved, where visitors can relive history by tossing "tea chests" into the ocean.

site of the nation's first public school, **Boston Latin** (1635), **Paul Revere's House** (c.1680), **King's Chapel** (1688, 1749), **Copp's Hill** and **Granary Burying Grounds** (1630, 1659 and 1660). Colonial sites from the **1700's**, many with important Royal and Revolutionary connections, are easily accessible by foot on the **Freedom Trail.** These include the **Old State House** (1713), the **Old Corner Book Store** (1718), the **Old North Church** (1723), the **Old South Meeting House** (1730), the **Boston Stone** (1737), **Faneuil Hall** (1742), and the **Boston Massacre Site** (1770). **The Freedom Trail Map** on page 25 shows the locations of these historic Boston sites.

Visitors will also enjoy exploring **Federalist Boston** from the **1800's**, especially the winding streets and brick townhouses of **Beacon Hill,** and the **U.S.S Constitution** (1797), docked at the **Charlestown Navy Yard**, as well as a distinctive neighborhoods of the **South End** and the **North End**.

The Freedom Trail

★ Boston's Freedom Trail starts at the **Boston Common** and winds 2.5 miles to **Bunker Hill** in Charlestown, past sixteen of Boston's most significant historic sites. The red painted pavement line or embedded brick path guides strollers through many neighborhoods reflecting different eras, from the 1600's through the 1800's. Like traveling in a time capsule, the walker experiences "Old Boston"–Puritan, Colonial, Revolutionary, Federal—and also traverses a variety of today's ethnic and cultural worlds, from Brahmin Beacon Hill to the Italian North End to Irish Charlestown.

Unlike a Disney theme park, "the sites along the Freedom Trail are not re-creations or adaptations. They are real. Each has its own special role in the beginning of a nation" (Freedom Trail Foundation).

Visitors should allow at least half a day to see the Freedom Trail sites in Boston and another half day to see those in Charlestown. Maps and information are available at Visitors Centers on the Boston Common and in the Prudential Center. Several excellent books describe each site in detail (see Sources).

Boston Historical Park

★ The Park is an "association of a number of sites that together provide a coherent view of the nation's history. Each site brings to life the American ideals of freedom of speech, religion, government, and self-determination." It is a cooperative venture with the city and private owners, since the Federal Government owns only three of the sites. There is much overlap with the Freedom Trail sites. One other important, but seldom visited site is **Dorchester Heights,** where the threat of bombardment of British war ships, anchored below in the Boston Harbor, from Colonial cannons hauled there surreptitiously, resulted in the total permanent evacuation of Boston by the British in 1776.

Faneuil Hall (1742) is called the "Cradle of Liberty," because American Patriots, often led by fiery Samuel Adams (statue), frequently met in the second floor Meeting Hall to protest British acts they found offensive, while customers shopped for food in the first floor Market.

The Old State House (1713) was the seat of Royal British authority in Massachusetts from where the Governor ruled and where the Massachusetts Assembly met until after the Revolution, in 1798.

The Park Visitors Center at 15 State Street, opposite the Old State House, features historic exhibits and a book shop. Park Rangers lead free regularly scheduled walks along the Freedom Trail.

Revolutionary Sites to See in Boston

★ Many of Boston's seventeenth and eighteenth century sites and their rich histories are intimately connected with the events of April 18-19, 1775, and visiting them will serve as a relevant preface to your subsequent visits to

★ BOSTON ★

Lexington and Concord and other Colonial towns west of Boston

★ **Boston Common** consists of 44 acres of open green space in the middle of Boston, that initially served as pasture land for Boston's (then called Shawmut) first white settler, Reverend William Blackstone in 1622. In 1630, Puritan settlers moved from Charlestown to seek the waters of an "Excellent Spring" in Boston. The "Common Land" was used for "feeding of cattell," as well as a "trayning field for militia."

During the occupation of Boston in the 1770s, British troops camped there. On the evening of April 18, 1775, about 700 British Redcoats assembled on the Common and, led by Lieutenant Colonel Francis Smith and Major John Pitcairn, embarked from a spot near today's **Public Gardens** at Charles Street and Boylston Street, then at the water's edge. They were ferried by boat across the Back Bay of the Charles River to Lechmere Point in Cambridge. Here the British Regulars began their twenty-four hour ordeal of marching westward to Concord and then eastward in rapid retreat from Concord back to Boston after the unexpected disastrous battles at Lexington and Concord.

★ **Paul Revere's House** in Boston's oldest neighborhood, the North End, was built around 1680 for a wealthy merchant. Today it is the oldest building still standing in Boston. Paul Revere (1735-1818) moved into the house in 1770, sired 16 children by his first wife, Sarah, and eight more by his second wife, Rachel. A well-respected silversmith and coppersmith, Revere was active in many patriotic groups in Boston and became an express rider in 1770, carrying patriots' messages to many other towns (Fischer). His 1775 gallop to Lexington was memorialized forever by Longfellow's poem, "The Midnight Ride of Paul Revere."

★ The **Old North Church**, just blocks from Revere's house, is Boston's oldest church. Officially named "Christ Church of Boston," it was built in 1723 and still functions actively as a church. On April 18, 1775, Revere's friend, sexton Robert Newman, hung two lanterns atop the steeple to signal to Patriots across the Charles River in Charlestown that the British troops were departing by boat across the river, not by land over the Boston Neck. (Today, one of the two original lanterns is displayed at the Concord Museum.) Revere was then rowed to Charlestown, where waiting Patriots gave him a horse to begin his famous Midnight Ride to alert the countryside west of Boston that, "The Regulars are out!"

Bunker Hill

"Don't fire until you see the whites of their eyes" is the legendary advice possibly given by Colonel William Prescott. Some believe that it may have been said by Colonel Israel Putnam. This comment was allegedly made on June 17, 1775 to the outnumbered Colonial defenders at Breed's Hill, at what later generations call the Battle of Bunker Hill. This statement symbolizes the "determination of the ill-equipped Colonists and marks the first time a unified Colonial Army took to the field against the powerful British Army"(Fleming).

Intrepid visitors today may climb the 294 steps (sorry, no elevator) leading to the top of the 221 foot-granite obelisk **Bunker Hill Monument** (1827-1842) that commemorates the battle. People less enthusiastic about exercising their aerobic stair-climbing prowess may visit the **Bunker Hill Lodge** at the monument's base and learn more about the battle by viewing historic dioramas and talking with knowledgeable Park Rangers.

To pre-empt a planned British attack on Colonial troops surrounding Boston, the Massachusetts Committee of Safety secretly ordered Colonial troops to fortify Bunker Hill, overlooking Boston Harbor. Several hundred volunteers from Massachusetts, Connecticut and New Hampshire spent the night of June 16 atop **Breed's Hill** hastily digging with their shovels to construct an earthen redoubt (fortification), 160 feet long by eighty feet wide, surrounded by walls six foot high and one foot thick and encircled by a deep ditch (moat) studded with fence rails and sticks. (Although the Committee of Safety originally ordered that the fort be built on the top of Bunker Hill, Connecticut's Colonel Putnam chose **Breed's Hill** instead, because it was closer to the Boston Harbor and thus more within the range of Colonial canons.)

The Old North Church (1723), (behind the Paul Revere statue) where sexton Robert Newman hung two lanterns to signal Patriots in Charlestown that British troops were being ferried "by sea," that is by water, not the land route across the Charles River late on the evening of April 18, 1775.

Bunker Hill Monument in Charlestown.

At day break, the watch of the British sloop Lively was astounded to see a brand new fort. British ships shelled it (with little effect). Enraged British officers, led by General William Howe met to plan immediate retaliation for the Colonists' impudent affront to their dominance.

The **first assault at Breed's Hill** by British Major General William Howe's Regulars began at 3:30 P.M., following an amphibious landing after the troops had been ferried in long boats from Boston to Moulton's Point on Charlestown's northern Mystic River shore. Angered by Colonial sniper fire, which harassed his invasion, General Howe ordered that the town of **Charlestown** be burned immediately in retribution. British cannons from the North Battery on Boston's Copp's Hill across the Harbor shelled Charlestown. The ensuing conflagration burned over 300 buildings to the ground, as spectators watched from the roofs of Boston.

Redcoats led by Brigadier General Robert Pigott attempted to breach wood fences and a stone wall, but were repulsed by the deadly musket fire of Colonial snipers. Colonial defenders also repealed a **second British assault**. The Regulars were hampered by being forced to carry over 100 pounds of equipment in the 80 degree heat and by attacking in field formations in scarlet uniforms, which made them easy targets.

However, the Colonists ammunition was almost expended and they were out-numbered and exhausted from their all–night exertions. On their costly **third assault** British soldiers cut through Colonial defenses and overran the earthen for-tification from three sides. The Colonists abandoned the fort and retreated north towards Cambridge. After two hours of savage combat, British troops had taken control of the Breed's Hill fortification and pursued the Americans only as far as Bunker's Hill, where they dug in.

"Victory" came with a stupendous price (as it always does in war). This bloody carnage cost the British an estimated 1054 casualties, about 40% of their total force of 2,200 invaders (207 men and 19 officers killed and 828 wounded). Marine Major Pitcairn, who had led the British columns to Lexington and Concord two months before, was killed. He was buried by his son.

Of the estimated 2,500 to 4000 Colonists, there were approximately 400-600 casualties (140 dead, 301 wounded and 30 taken prisoner) (Fleming). A grave American loss was the death of Dr. Joseph Warren, who was a physician and Patriot leader, as well as a brave soldier.

"Only gradually did Americans begin to see Bunker Hill as a kind of victory. One of the first to reach this conclusion was a young Rhode Island general, Nathaniel Greene: 'I wish we could sell them another hill at the same price,' he said. Today we know that the battle crippled the British Army and threw it on the defensive for more than a year" (Fleming).

Sources:
Bahne, Charles, Complete Guide to Boston's Freedom Trail, 1993.
Booth, Robert, Boston's Freedom Trail, Globe Pequot Press, 1994.
Boston Museum of Fine Arts, Paul Revere's Boston, 1735-1818, 1975.
Boston National Historical Park, Boston and the American Revolution;
    Bunker Hill; Freedom Trail (Map). 1998.
Fleming, Thomas, Liberty! The American Revolution, Viking, 1997 (also on P.B.S. Tape).
Freedom Trail Foundation, Boston's Freedom Trail: Map and Guide, 1998.
Hogarth, Paul, Walking Tours of Old Boston, Dutton, 1978.
Jennings, John, Boston: Cradle of Liberty, 1630-1776, Doubleday, 1947.
Linden, Blanche, Boston Freedom Trail, Back Bay Press, 1996.
Massachusetts Historical Society, Colonial Boston, 1976; The Changing
    Face of Boston Over 350 Years, Boston, 1980.
Schofield, William G., Freedom By The Bay: Boston Freedom Trail, 1974.
Weston, George F., Boston Ways: High, By, and Folk, Beacon Press. 1957.
Whitehill, Walter M., Boston: A Topographical History, Harvard University, 1968.
Wilson, Dana L., Boston English Illustrated, Centennial Press, 1976.

★ ★ ★ ★

The British in Boston: Regulars, Redcoats and Lobster Backs

BY JAY CANNON

Today when we hear about the "shot heard around the world," we often think about the American citizen-soldier leaving his farm in 1775 to do battle against fighting men from the mighty British Empire. But who were these British soldiers? Who were these fighting men Americans called "Regulars", "lobster backs", and "Redcoats"? Who were these men from England who in the words of poet James Russell Lowell, carved on the stone tomb of two Redcoats who were slain at the Battle at Concord's North Bridge, "Came three thousand miles and died/To keep the past upon its throne?"

When the British Parliament passed the Townshend Acts in 1767, citizens of Boston resented the new restrictions on their liberties and the new import tax. They started a campaign of harassment of British government officials living in Boston. The military Governor of Massachusetts, General Thomas Gage, fearing the situation was getting out of control, requested that more British troops be

British Redcoats from His Majesty's 10th Regiment of Foot; modern re-eenactors relive April 19,1775.

Fifers and drummers lead His Majesty's 10th Regiment of Foot on the Battle Road in Lincoln.

stationed in Boston. His request was honored. On September 30, 1768 four thousand fresh British troops landed from ships which were anchored in the Boston Harbor. Shortly thereafter, the troops were quartered with the local residents, against their will. Some soldiers set up tents in Boston Common, since housing was in short supply.

Because of frequent confrontations with American Patriots, British tempers flared. General Gage received reports that British guns and powder were being stolen and hoarded by rebellious Yankees in the surrounding countryside. He routinely organized troop maneuvers, in which British troops marched into the nearby Massachusetts towns to investigate the rumors that townspeople were stockpiling and hiding munitions. The town of Salem was the target of one such foray by King George's Regulars on February 26, 1775. The Redcoats reached Salem, but found no hidden weapons there.

During the winter of 1774-75, the Committee of Safety of the First Provincial Congress, which met at the First Parish Church in Concord, voted that arms, enough to support and army of fifteen thousand men, be collected and stored in Concord. Since Concord is eighteen miles from Boston, the Patriots felt their hidden weapons would be out of reach of General Gage's troops. But Gage, being an astute commander, received accurate information about the exact hiding spots for the Concord weapons stores from the military spies he sent into the countryside.

Hoping for a quick pre-emptive strike at Concord, on April 18, 1775, General Gage ordered Lieutenant Colonel Francis Smith to muster some 700-900 men to prepare for a march from Boston to seize the Concord stores. These men were among the most elite British troops stationed in Boston. They consisted mainly of

Grenadier and Light Infantry companies. Grenadier's were reputed to be fearless, large and forbidding men, who wore tall bear skin caps. They were so named, because earlier in the century, they had been equipped to hurl bombs or grenades against the enemy. By the latter part of the eighteenth century grenadiers traded in their hand bombs for muskets, but continued to earn their reputation as among the most fearless fighters in the British forces. The men of the Light Infantry, better known as the "Lights", were just as

Redcoat re-enactors with muskets in Lincoln woods.

fearless, but were generally smaller in build. Their job was to patrol on each side of the main marching column to prevent attacks from either side, as "flankers", that is to patrol from the flanks. They often marched through trees and undergrowth; thus they needed to more nimble.

Most of the men who made up the British Army were from Wales, Ireland, Scotland and England. Many joined of their own free will, but as time went on and manpower became scarce, forced enrollment or conscription became more common. One problem with the use of conscripted men was that the desertion rate was high. Estimates place the number of British soldiers who deserted at more than 10% throughout the war. Some British deserters were shot on the Boston Common in plain view of their comrades and the Boston public. This often added to the feeling of the Boston citizens that the British military men were cruel and heartless.

Early on the morning of April 9, 1775, Colonel Francis Smith commanded the British troops that had crossed the Charles River by boat from Boston to Cambridge. They then departed from Cambridge with the objective of capturing hidden military stores in Concord. Under Lieutenant Colonel Smith's command, Major John Pitcairn of the Royal Marines commanded eleven regiments of troops, totaling over 700 men.

Some notable facts about the British Expedition to Concord

★ The senior British officer at the North Bridge confrontation was Captain Laurie of the 43rd Foot Light Infantry. After the Battle of Bunker Hill, Captain Laurie buried the American leader, Dr. Joseph Warren's body with another "rebel" and remarked of his burial "... his seditious principles may remain."

★ Captain Lawrence Parsons, 10th Foot, Light Infantry, after leaving Captain Laurie in charge at the North Bridge, led his troops two miles to the Barrett farm to search for and seize weapons British spies had previously informed him were hidden there. Upon his return to the North Bridge he and his men marched past the many Colonials who were unharmed after the brief battle at the North Bridge. Captain Parsons was wounded later that day as the British retreated from Concord towards Boston along the Battle Road. Six weeks later he was wounded again at Bunker Hill.

★ Lieutenant Colonel Francis Smith, leader of the British expedition, 10th Foot, was wounded on the British retreat from Concord to Boston. Smith eventually rose to the rank of Major General in the British Army.

★ Major John Pitcairn, commander of the Redcoats at the Lexington Green, died months later of wounds received at Bunker Hill from a musket ball fired by African-American militiaman, Salem Peter. Pitcairn's own son carried his father off the field.

★ Of the seventy-four British officers who marched to Concord, thirty-three were either killed or severely wounded between April 19, 1775 and the Battle of Bunker Hill on June 17, 1775.

★ About the Battle of Bunker Hill (actually Breed's Hill), British General Burgoyne, commenting on the heavy British losses, to capture the hill, wrote, "The Fifth (Regiment) has behaved the best, but suffered to most."

★ The British made up the tune "Yankee Doodle" and intended it as an insult to the Americans. After their totally unexpected successes during the fighting at Concord and Lexington, Americans were proud to be called "Yankee Doodle."

Sources:
Fischer, David H., Paul Revere's Ride, Oxford, 1994.
Ketchem, R. (Editor), The American Heritage Book of the American Revolution, Simon and Schuster, 1958.
Fleming, Thomas, Liberty, The American Revolution, 1997.
    (Video tape available, from P.B.S.).
Fusiliers Museum of Northumberland, The Royal Regiment of Fusiliers,
    ("5th Regiment of Foot"), Morpeth, Northumberland, 1998.

★ ★ ★ ★

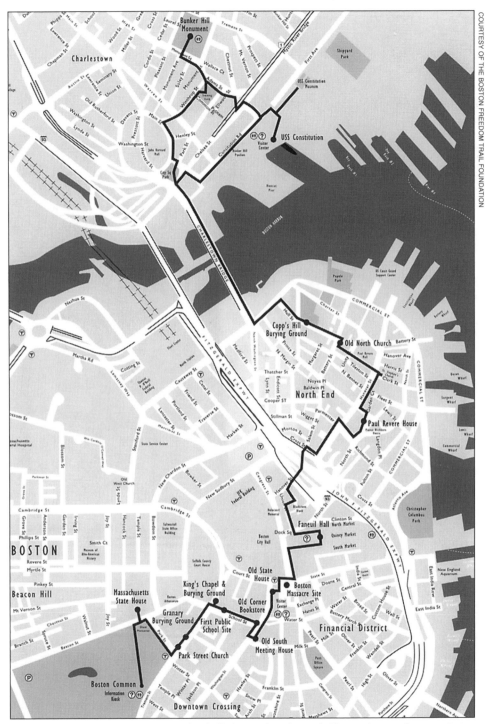

The Boston Freedom Trail, is a walking trail that highlights significant historic buildings and sites in downtown Boston and Charlestown.

★ ★ ★ ★

Old Burying Ground, Cambridge

★ ★ ★ ★

Cambridge: Puritans, Patriots, Tories and Scholars

 ambridge's roles in the American Revolution were as varied as the lives of the people who lived there in the 1770's. Over 90% of Cambridge's approximately 2000 residents then were descendents of the 700 Puritans, who had sailed from England in eleven ships in 1630. They had settled on the north bank of the Charles River, eight miles upstream from Boston. Their dream—and their deed—was to build a community that was purer and closer to the Bible than those they left behind in England.

In **Newtowne** (re-named Cambridge in 1638 after England's university town) they laid out an orderly grid of streets which ran down to the river. Each family owned a modest house in the village, farmed their planting fields on the outskirts of town and shared common land for grazing livestock. Basically the Puritans re-created the pattern of the English villages they had left behind, as also occurred in most other New England towns. Shortly thereafter they built a meeting house (church), a school and a marketplace (Brief History).

In 1636 they founded the first college in North America to train young men for

COURTESY OF THE CAMBRIDGE HISTORICAL SOCIETY

George Washington assumes command of the Continental Army on the Cambridge Common, on July 3, 1775.

★ CAMBRIDGE ★

the (Puritan) ministry and to be godly citizens. They named it in honor of the Charlestown minister, who donated his library of several hundred books and half his estate. His name was John Harvard.

By the 1770's descendents of these original Puritan farmers and clergymen were farmers, artisans (blacksmiths, carpenters, shoemakers, tailors, coopers, saddlers,) merchants and a few were purveyors of new services i.e. lawyers, distillers, and counting house men. These men had few outside economic resources; instead they relied completely on the local economy. As crises about taxes and political control escalated in the 1770's, by and large, these men opposed the Crown. They supported local interests and called for more local autonomy from London. Lacking meaningful ties to King George III or his Royal Representatives in the Commonwealth of Massachusetts, they became Patriots. They were willing to sacrifice a secure, but subservient, future for the promise of more political, social and economic freedom that they hoped independence from Britain would bring (Bunting).

A smaller group of wealthy families who settled in large country estates in Cambridge were "Loyalist, oligarchic and Anglican." They either descended from the few Puritan families, like the Brattles and the Foxcrofts, who had acquired wealth and subsequently lost their Puritan ways, or, like the Phipsess and the Vassals, had substantial income which originated from outside of Cambridge. They prospered on income, either from plantations in the West Indies, from profitable mercantile businesses in Boston or from payments for services rendered to the King. Cambridge Loyalists worshipped at their own Anglican church, Christ Church. They gave lavish parties, planted lush gardens in lieu of farming, socialized mostly with each other and frequently intermarried. Most of these few elite families clustered in spacious mansions with extensive grounds on the Watertown Road in the west end of Cambridge, later named **Brattle Street**, then as now also called **"Tory Row"** (Bunting). Several other Tory families lived on huge estates on the eastern shore of Fresh Pond (Krim).

These Cambridge Tories led the good life, but not for long. By accepting Royal favors, supporting the Crown and rejecting the rebels, they hoped to keep their special privileges and maintain their aristocratic status quo. Unfortunately for them, when the Revolution started after the battles of Lexington and Concord and after Bunker Hill in 1775, the provisional government confiscated most Tory estates.

The newly homeless Loyalists were forced to flee, many of them departing with the British fleet. They headed first for Halifax, Nova Scotia and from thence back to England.

Ironically, Loyalists' luxurious houses were used as barracks for farmer – soldiers who gathered from rustic country towns. They joined the fledgling Continental Army, then encamped in Cambridge. The Vassal mansion on Brattle Street (today called Longfellow House) became General George Washington's headquarters during the Siege of Boston in 1775-1776.

★ CAMBRIDGE ★

Cambridge's first direct contact with the coming conflict occurred late in the evening of April 18 and early on the morning of April 19, 1775. Williams Dawes galloped over the Boston Neck, through Roxbury and along **Cambridge's Great Road** (today's Massachusetts Avenue) to alert the countryside that British troops were advancing to Concord to seize hidden weapons. Several hours later 700 British Regulars under Lieutenant Colonel Francis Smith were ferried across the Charles River to land below the Phips farm at **Lechmere's Point in East Cambridge**. After a delay in the swampy landing spot, at about 2 A.M. Smith finally led his men westward from Cambridge along the Great Road towards Lexington, then Concord.

British General Thomas Gage had ordered a second expedition of about 1000 fresh troops under Brigadier General Hugh Percy to be sent from Boston towards Concord to relieve Smith's exhausted and depleted Regulars. This relief force did not leave Boston until after daybreak (after the clashes between Smith's Redcoats and Colonial militia and Minutemen at Lexington Green and Concord's North Bridge had both finished.) Percy's troops marched over the land route via Roxbury. They were delayed further due to sabotage to the **Great Bridge** by local Patriots and did not reach Cambridge until mid-morning. They did not rendezvous with Colonel Smith's exhausted, retreating soldiers in Lexington until about 3 P.M. (Krim).

The combined British forces of Smith and Percy, now totalling about 1700 men, "had little choice but to return along the **Great Road** (through Menotomy— today's Arlington— and Cambridge). The Road was bristling with Minutemen, militia and farmers awaiting an opportunity to harass the Redcoats" (Krim). Trying to avoid certain ambush in Cambridge town, Percy led his regiment to the left fork, the road to Charlestown.

Percy's flankers discovered three rebels, crouching behind dry casks in Jacob Watson's yard. The Redcoats killed all three Cambridge men, Major Isaac Gardner, John Hicks and Moses Richardson. For good measure, they also killed William Marcy, a simpleminded bystander, who had turned out to watch a parade.

Percy, using his cannons, shelled the militia men massed further down the **Cambridge Road**, and, "under the cover of his fire, the column marched past the danger point and on towards Charlestown." When they staggered over the **Charlestown Neck** and climbed up to the safety of **Bunker Hill,** it was past 7 P.M. and dark. From Charlestown the exhausted British soldiers, many wounded, were ferried back to Boston during the night by Royal Navy long boats (Galvin).

Immediately following the British debacles at Lexington and Concord, thousands of Colonial Minutemen and militia, who had arrived in the area from all over New England, surrounded Boston peninsula and its 5,000 occupying British troops under General Gage. This Siege of Boston was to last for nine months, from April 19, 1775 to March 17, 1776. The Provincials cut off all possible land transportation and escape routes, forcing the British to rely on the Royal Navy for supplies and reinforcements.

★ CAMBRIDGE ★

The approximately 15,000 men in the Colonial Army, under the command of Massachusetts General Artemis Ward, were a rag tag collection of loosely organized, minimally trained and poorly equipped volunteers. Many of them, anxious to return to their farms for the spring planting, later defected before their enlistments were up. The disastrous Battle of Bunker Hill on June 17 (see Boston chapter) left them even more dispirited.

On June 14, eight weeks after Lexington and Concord and three weeks before Bunker Hill, the Continental Congress in Philadelphia elected Virginia's militia Colonel George Washington to be General. He was to replace Ward as Commander of the disjointed bands of New England militia surrounding Boston, now to be called the Continental Army. John Adams, seconded by his cousin Samuel Adams, had proposed Washington, much to the chagrin of their fellow Massachusetts delegate, the presiding official, John Hancock, who had coveted the Commanding General appointment for himself (Fleming).

Washington arrived in Cambridge on July 3 to assume command of the newly designated Continental Army. It is doubtful that he assumed command and surveyed 9000 assembled militia men, in an elaborate ceremony under the spreading elm on the **Cambridge Common**, as local legend has it. This famous scene, never substantiated, was depicted in many subsequent illustrations, and added mythical stature to the already impressive reality of the modest, yet ambitious farmer-soldier-statesman who was George Washington (Batchelder, Rees).

What Washington did find in Cambridge was, in his words, "a mixed multitude of people...under very little discipline, order, or government" (Ketchum). The disparate men who were to form his new Continental Army lacked training or money for pay. They were short of tents, blankets, sanitary facilities, muskets, powder, ammunition and bayonets. They did not have firm commitments for fixed terms of enlistment and served only according to their whim of the moment, so their very presence for future action was tenuous. For the intriguing story of how Washington molded undisciplined mobs of men into an effective fighting force, I commend you to other authors (Washington, Ketchum, Fleming). It is a story worth reading, to understand with deeper insight the Colonists' unlikely ultimate victory against the once dominant British. And it all began in Cambridge.

Revolutionary Sites to Visit in Cambridge

★ **The Cambridge Common** (1631), a triangular park between Massachusetts Avenue, Garden and Waterhouse Streets, has been the focal point for Cambridge's economic, social, religious and political life for over 350 years. According to legend (see text and illustration), on July 3, 1775 under a spreading elm George Washington took command of 9000 men, who were to form the newly created Continental Army. A plaque on the Garden Street side of the Common commemorates the event most historians believe is more myth than reality. During the Siege of Boston in 1775 and 1776 the Common served as the main camping ground for the tents of General Washington's Continental Army. Plaques on the **Commons' entry gateways** celebrate Washington's stay in Cambridge.

★ **The Cambridge Burying Ground** (1635) is situated between First Parish and Christ Churches on Garden Street. The slate head stones illustrate changing fashions in tombstone sculpture, from medieval death's heads of the late 1600's to Renaissance-inspired winged cherubs of the 1700's to Neoclassical urn-and-willow mourning motifs of the early 1800's. "From realistic to symbolic they thus chronicle changing attitudes towards death" (Bunting).

★ **Christ Church** (1761), on Garden Street, designed by architect Peter Harrison, is the oldest church in Cambridge. Its congregants were wealthy Anglican Loyalists. When its Tory members departed from Cambridge in 1775, Connecticut militiamen used the church as their barracks. They melted the organ pipes for bullets. George and Martha Washington worshipped here during their stay in Cambridge.

★ **Harvard University** (1636) still has original buildings that were standing, when William Dawes galloped over the nearby Great Road (Massachusetts Avenue) towards Lexington, alarming the countryside on April 18, 1775. British troops advancing to and then retreating from Concord marched by Harvard on the same route.

Wadsworth House (1727) at 1341 Massachusetts Avenue and **Harvard Square**, was built as the official residence of Harvard presidents and served this purpose for nine presidents until 1849. When George Washington first arrived in Cambridge in 1775, it served briefly as his house and headquarters.

A walk around the **Harvard Yard**, off of Harvard Square, takes the visitor past some of Harvard's most historic buildings. The oldest Harvard building, **Massachusetts Hall** (1720) now houses both administrators and freshman dormitories. During the Revolution it served as barracks for Continental Army soldiers. Other Colonial Harvard buildings include **Holden Chapel** (1744), **Harvard Hall** (1642, 1764) and **Hollis Hall** (1763).

Many college buildings were appropriated as housing by Continental Army soldiers during the Revolution, which displaced students. Therefore, Harvard College moved temporarily from Cambridge to Concord in October, 1775. Harvard's move west was mostly due to the efforts of Ralph Waldo Emerson's grandfather, Concord minister Reverend William Emerson (both were Harvard graduates). After volunteering to serve as Army chaplain, William Emerson died of "camp fever" the same year, on the road accompanying American soldiers who were marching through Vermont to capture Fort Ticonderoga on Lake Champlain (Wheeler).

★ **Longfellow National Historic Site** (Vassal-Craigie-Longfellow House, 1759) is an imposing large yellow Colonial mansion on "Tory Row" at 105 Brattle Street. It was originally the home of wealthy plantation owner John Vassall, Jr., whose Loyalists sentiments prompted him to flee to England during the Revolution after the provisional government expropriated his house. George Washington used it is his headquarters in 1775-6. Here he and Martha celebrated their 17th wedding anniversary in January, 1776. Because former owner Andrew Craigie's insolvent widow was forced to take in boarders, in 1836, Henry Wadsworth Longfellow, a young Harvard professor, rented a room from widow Craigie. Longfellow later received the house as a wedding gift from the father of his bride, Fanny Appleton. The couple led a productive life, raising six children during their 45 years as residents. Longfellow's epic poems gave hin international fame. Longfellow House is operated by the National Park Service and is open to the public at regular hours and for special programs. Entry is free.

★ Other Brattle Street "Tory Row" houses include the **Henry Vassall House** (c. 1630's) at 94 Brattle Street and the **William Brattle House** (1727) at number 42. These houses are privately owned and not open to the public.

Sources:
Batchelder, Samuel F., The Washington Elm Tradition, Cambridge Tribune, 1925.
Bunting, Bainbridge & Nylander, Robert, Old Cambridge, Cambridge Historical Commission.
Cambridge Historical Commission, A Brief History of Cambridge, 1999.
Fleming, Thomas, Liberty! The American Revolution, Viking, 1997.
Galvin, John R., The Minutemen, The First Fight: Myths and Realities of the American Revolution, Brassey's, 1967 & 1989.
Harvard University, A Self-Guided Walking Tour of the Harvard Yard, 1998.
Ketchum, Richard M., The World of George Washington, American Heritage, 1974.
Krim, Arthur J., Northwest Cambridge, Cambridge Historical Commission, 1977.
Longfellow National Historic Site, informational materials, 1999.
Okie, Susan & Yee Donna (Editors), Boston Bicentennial Guidebook, Dutton, 1975.
Rees, James C., opening of "George Washington: Portrait of a Patriot," sponsored by Mount Vernon Ladies' Association, Concord Museum, March 12, 1999.
Washington, George, Maxims, Reprinted by Mount Vernon Ladies' Association, 1989.
Wheeler, Ruth R., Concord: Climate for Freedom, 1967.

★ ★ ★ ★

Battle Road's Most Savage Fighting Forgotten: The Story of Menotomy (Arlington)

BY D. MICHAEL RYAN

O n the 19th of April, 1775, British troops were dispatched by Governor and Commanding General Thomas Gage. They marched, heading westward toward Concord, to seize hidden American arms. Some four miles from Boston they reached a village called Menotomy. ('Menotomy' is Native American for 'Swift Running Waters.' The town was once named 'West Cambridge' and is now called 'Arlington'). As the British troops marched through the streets of Menotomy at about 3 A.M. on the morning of April 19th, generally all appeared quiet. Such would not be true later in the afternoon when the Redcoats returned.

Colonel Francis Smith's British column paused at **Menotomy Center**, near the Black Horse Tavern, which previously had hosted the illegal Provincial Committees of Safety and Supplies. A hungry British patrol had eaten there the previous day. British Major John Pitcairn was ordered to proceed with six com-

Menotomy Minute Men and British Redcoats re-enact the fierce fighting at the Jason Russell House, in Arlington (Menotomy).

panies to secure the bridges in Concord. These Light Infantry units later encountered and fired upon Captain John Parker's Lexington militia on the Lexington Green. By dawn, twenty-three of the fifty-three Menotomy Minutemen in Captain Benjamin Locke's company mustered and marched toward Lexington. Throughout the day, they would engage the King's soldiers at many points along the **Battle Road**.

By noon, following the deadly dawn skirmishes in Lexington and Concord, Colonel Smith's British forces began the long march back to Boston, harassed all along the way by Provincials. As his men were being battered at **The Bloody Curve in Lincoln** (at 1:30 p.m.), British Brigadier General Hugh, Lord Percy's relief brigade, previously summoned by a desperate Lt. Colonel Smith from Boston, was passing through a peaceful Menotomy. Somewhat behind the soldiers came two supply wagons, rushing to catch the column. They were ambushed by twelve Menotomy "old men," who had been left behind, because it was felt that they were unsuited for regular military duty. They were led by a half-Indian named David Lamson. These "old men" killed two British guards, wounded another, and captured some British supplies.

Fleeing British soldiers threw their muskets into **Spy Pond**, then surrendered to an old woman digging dandelions, Mother Ruth Bathericke. She presented her prisoners to a militia officer and informed the Redcoats, "If you ever live to get back, you tell King George that an old woman took six of his Grenadiers prisoners." In England, newspapers asked, "If one old Yankee woman can take six Grenadiers, how many soldiers will it require to conquer America?"

The fleeing British soldiers of Colonel Smith and the reinforcements from Boston led by General Percy joined together in Lexington to form a formidable British force. They resumed their march together eastward toward Boston, entering Menotomy at about 4:30 p.m. near **Foot of the Rocks** (Arlington Heights). American General William Heath and Dr. Joseph Warren had arrived in the field in an attempt to organize the Colonials. Now the most savage, deadly, and intense combat of the day commenced, as some 1,700 Redcoats faced some 2,000 Provincials in thirty-five companies from Middlesex, Essex and Norfolk counties in Massachusetts.

While the Colonials fought independently and with minimal organization, the Regulars struggled to maintain discipline and order. Scared, tired, and angry, the British soldiers lost control, burning and looting houses they believed had been used by Colonials to fire upon them. Hannah Adams, baby in her arms and children under her bed, was assaulted at bayonet point, but released. Her children managed to extinguish a fire set by the Redcoats. The Robbins and Cutler homes were vandalized and torched, and church silver was stolen.

Individual combat took place. Dr. Eliphalet Downer of Roxbury crossed bayonets with a Redcoat and killed him. Lieutenant Bowman of Menotomy caught a British straggler, clubbed him to the ground, and captured him. Samuel Whittemore, age 80, hid behind a wall with a musket, two pistols, and a sword.

Upon being approached by British flankers, he killed two and wounded one before being knocked unconscious by a musketball to his head. Battered, bayoneted, and left for dead by the soldiers, he was reluctantly treated by Dr. Cotton Tufts, who believed the injured man could not survive. Whittemore, however, lived to the age of 98.

The most savage combat of the day took place at the **farm house of Jason Russell.** Age 58 and lame, Russell had refused to flee, noting that "an Englishman's house is his castle." When surprised by a British flanking party, a group of Colonials sought refuge in Russell's house. Russell was too slow to escape and was

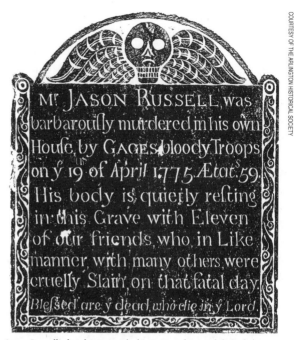

Jason Russell's headstone marks his resting place and that of eleven other Minutemen who lost their lives in the single bloodiest fight of the first day of the American Revolution in Arlington.

shot twice at his doorway, then bayoneted eleven time by pursuing Redcoats. He was killed in his own doorway. Inside and about the building, thirteen Provincials died, including seven from Danvers and four from Lynn. Two Regulars were killed. Eight Colonials saved themselves by hiding in the cellar, which the Redcoats dared not enter. Mrs. Russell, upon returning home, noted bodies piled about the floor and blood ankle deep.

At **Cooper's Tavern**, the owner Benjamin Cooper and his wife fled to the cellar as the British soldiers approached. However, two unarmed non-combatants, believing themselves safe from harm, continued drinking their ale. Jason Winship and Jabez Wyman were bayoneted to death, "their heads mauled, their skulls broken, and their brains scattered about the floor and walls."

Just after 6 p.m., as the sun set in the west, the British column passed quietly out of the war-torn, smoldering Menotomy into **Cambridge**. During the one and a half hours along the almost two miles of the Menotomy Road, unimaginable horrors occurred, accounting for almost half of the day's casualties on both sides. Twenty-eight Americans of the total of the 49 killed that day along the Battle Road were slain in Menotomy. Ten more were wounded, out of the total of 41 wounded in combat that day.

Forty Redcoats were killed out of the total of 73 killed along the Battle Road, and 80 were wounded out of the approximately 174 total British soldiers wounded on that day.

The twelve Colonials killed at the Russell house were buried in a mass grave behind the **First Parish Church**. British Lieutenant Edward Gould, wounded in Concord, was captured in Menotomy. Lieutenant Edward Hall, also wounded in Concord, was again hit and died in the village. He was treated by Mrs. Butterfield, who was called a Tory, but later defended her act of humanity. Lieutenant Joseph Knight died of wounds received in town. One British soldier noted, "We were most annoyed at a village called Anatomy...houses were all full of men."

Menotomy (later to be named Arlington), bled and burned in the fury of the battle on the 19th of April, 1775, as its citizens spilled their own blood to defend their ideals and to help begin a revolution. Then, it quietly disappeared into history, overshadowed by the other more famous events that day at Concord and Lexington. Prophetically, the grand-daughter of Jason Russell, who was slain, was born in Menotomy Village, on that same fateful day and on the next Sabbath the infant son of Jason Winship was baptized. After all the carnage of April 19, a new generation was being born to help assure Menotomy's future.

Revolutionary War Sites to Visit Today in Arlington (Previously called Menotomy)

Jason Russell House in Arlington (Menotomy).

★ **The Jason Russell House (1740) and Smith History Museum** at 7 Jason St. near Massachusetts Ave and Route 60 is operated by the Arlington Historical Society and is open to the public at specified times. It was the site of fierce hand to hand combat during the British retreat to Boston. Now it houses 18th century furniture and artifacts, as well as changing exhibits about the Revolutionary War.

★ **First Parish Church and Burial Ground** at 638 Massachusetts Avenue near Route 60 is open to the public.

★ **Spy Pond**, where the fleeing British troops tossed their muskets, provided cut ice later in the 1830s, which was shipped to help to cool distant tropical countries as distant as India. It can be viewed from Route 2 driving west or Route 60 driving north.

★ **Foot of the Rocks** at the corner of Lowell and Massachusetts Avenues in Arlington Heights is marked by boulders with plaques, commemorating the spot where the deadliest combat occurred on April 19, 1775 between retreating British troops and American soldiers from over 30 neighboring towns.

★ **Capt. Benjamin Locke's House** at 21 Appleton St. in Arlington Heights and

COURTESY OF THE MENOTOMY MINUTE MEN

Menotomy Minute Men parade through Arlington on Patriots' Day.

The Whittemore House at 54 Massachusetts Avenue in East Arlington, previously housed the families of participants in the Menotomy skirmish. The houses are now privately owned and not open to the public.

★ **The Minute Man Bike Trail**, originally an abandoned rail line, starts in East Arlington and runs 11.2 miles through Lexington to Bedford. It is popular with cyclists and strollers in the summer and with cross country skiers, when snow falls.

★ **The Menotomy Minute Men,** this 1775 group was re-organized in 1971 to perpetuate the memory and achievements of the original company through living history reenactments, educational programs and promotion of civic events. The company consists of musketeers, a fife and drum corps and the Menotomy Boys and Girls groups. Membership is open to interested individuals and families.

Sources:
Smith, Samuel, West Cambridge 1775, 1974.
First National Bank of Boston, The Lexington-Concord Battle Road, 1975.
French, Allen, The Day of Concord and Lexington, 1925.

This famous **Minuteman Statue in Lexington** (1900) depicts Capt. John Parker at the Battle of Lexington. It is located at the triangular shaped Lexington Green.

Lexington: Where the Green Flowed Red

Lexingtonians retain great pride in their unique Revolutionary history. Many original houses and several taverns, important in the events of 1775, still stand here. Knowlegeable area professionals and volunteers act as guides and offer a friendly welcome to visitors from around the world.

An excellent way to begin your visit to Lexington is to stop at the **Lexington Visitors' Center** across from the Lexington Green. Here you can get information about the many important area historic houses and sites to visit, most of them within a short walking distance. You can also learn current information about local museums, restaurants, hotels and special exhibits and historical and cultural programs in the area. The Gift Shop features souvenirs and books relevant to Lexington's rich history. The Visitors' Center is operated by the Lexington Chamber of Commerce.

Lexington today is a lively, upscale residential community of about 30,000 people. Its main street (**Massachusetts Avenue**) is lined with a variety of traditional gracious Colonial houses and stores, as well as newer red brick shops, ranging from book stores to antique shops to American and ethnic restaurants. In the summer visitors can enjoy dinner or an ice cream cone in an outdoor café or relax on a sidewalk bench and enjoy the passing parade of locals and visitors.

Because of their proximity to Boston and to the many area "hi tech" companies,

COURTESY OF THE LEXINGTON HISTORICAL SOCIETY

The Boulder on the Green marks the position of the 77-man company of Minutemen at the site of the clash of arms in 1775. The inscription is a quote attributed to Captain John Parker.

universities and cultural institutions and because of the excellent public and private schools, Lexington, as well as Concord and the other historic suburbs featured in this book, are highly regarded as residential communities. All these Boston area suburban towns encompass many neighborhoods with beautiful houses, in both traditional Colonial and modern styles. Wooded parks, numerous rivers, ponds, lakes, conservation areas, recreational facilities and unique historic sites add to the desirability both of living in and visiting these towns.

Many residents of Lexington and neighboring towns along with visitors arise early each **Patriot's Day** (near April 19) to watch 6 A.M. ceremonies on the **Lexington Battle Green**. Modern incarnations of Minutemen and Redcoats face each other across the Green, re-enacting the historic confrontations of their fore-fathers. They fire musket "shots" at the opposing troops. After the gun smoke clears, slain Patriots and Redcoats alike arise from their lifeless forms on the ground, stand upright and then walk once more. Then together erstwhile enemies march in a grand Patriots' Day Parade and join the celebrations together at festive Patriots' Day parties.

Lexington Battle Green (also called Lexington Common). In 1712 citizens of Cambridge Commons (later Lexington) purchased 1 1/2 acres of land next to the Meeting House (church) for town common land, which was later enlarged by one acre.

In 1775 the Green was a scrubby cow pasture in the center of town. **The Belfry Bell** summoned about 130 men from Capt. John Parker's Lexington militia to the Green at about 12:30 AM on April 19. A **boulder** engraved with a musket and powder horn marks the spot where Sergeant William Munroe's men mustered and formed their line. At about 1:30 A.M. Captain Parker dismissed his men, and many retreated to **Buckman Tavern** for some liquid refreshments.

At about 4:30 AM, when a scout reported to Captain John Parker that columns

The Lexington Minute Man is located on the eastern tip on Lexington Green.

This oil by Henry Sandham (1886) depicts the confrontation between the Minutemen and British troops on **Lexington Common**, April 19, 1775 at about 5 a.m. Most historians doubt the historical accuracy of this depiction, since according to depositions of the participants, most American militiamen were "dispersing" (retreating), not lining up to fire at the British. The painting is in the collection of the Lexington Historical Society and hangs in Cary Memorial Town Hall.

of marching Redcoats were almost in Lexington, drummer boy William Diamond beat his drum to recall the militiamen. About 77 Lexington militiamen reassembled to form two rows on the northeast side of the triangular Green. The men ranged from a grandfather, Jonas Parker, Captain Parker's cousin, to Jonathan Harrington whose house faced the Green, to a black slave, Prince Estabrook, who had volunteered and been voted into the militia, to teenagers William Diamond and Isaac Muzzy. They had been anxiously awaiting the British troops' arrival all night.

They suddenly faced an advance column of about 300 British light infantry, led by Royal Marine Major John Pitcairn, who approached the Lexington Green from the southeast, having just marched from Cambridge and Menotomy (Arlington). They were to be followed shortly by over 400 more Grenadiers, led by their portly, slow moving but experienced commander, Lieutenant Colonel Francis Smith.

Captain John Parker did not want an armed confrontation between his small band and the over 700 British British Regulars who were rapidly marching directly towards them. Not wanting to risk reckless suicidal gun fire by blocking the British columns, Captain Parker first ordered his men, as Paul Revere overheard and stated in a later deposition, to "Let the troops pass by" (Revere). Parker added, "Don't molest them, without they being first (to fire)."

One of his men, William Munroe, swore in a deposition in 1822, almost 50 years after the event, that he heard Captain Parker assert: "Stand your ground! Don't fire unless fired upon! But if they want to have a war, let it begin here!" This has become part of local mythology and is even engraved in stone on the Green (Fischer).

Whether or not Captain Parker ever actually uttered this reputed defiant challenge as the Regulars came closer, is a matter of speculation. Many modern historians are doubtful of the veracity of this remark, attributed to Captain Parker. In addition to the absence of accounts by contemporary witnesses, they point out that it is unlikely that Captain Parker could have anticipated or desired an armed confrontation, when all the previous British expeditions into the countryside near Boston to intimidate the Colonists had concluded without gun fire. It is more likely that a veteran of the clash, with a less than total-recall memory fifty years after the event, tended to glorify his leader's statements (Sideris).

The British vanguard was led by Marine Lieutenant Jesse Adair, an Irishman with a reputation as an aggressive officer. As he approached the triangular **Lexington Green**, with his more experienced superior officers Major Pitcairn and Lieutenant Colonel Smith marching behind him, he had to make a quick decision. A large Meeting House (church), then stood on the easternmost angle of the Green (where the Lexington Minuteman stands today, still facing in the direction of the British).

A long roll of this **drum** by 16-year-old William Diamond rallied Lexington's militiamen Minutemen on Lexington Common on the morning of April 19, 1775. The **pistols** were captured from British Major John Pitcairn of the Royal Marines later that same day. Both are now displayed at the **Hancock-Clarke** House.

The road from Cambridge (today's **Massachusetts Avenue**) forked around both sides of the church. The left fork leads west to Concord and the right fork goes to Bedford to the northeast.

Lieutenant Adair's snap decision was to take the right fork, the Bedford Road, perhaps to avoid leaving the right flank of his column exposed to the assembled militia on the northeast portion of the Green, as he would have done had he chosen the Concord Road (Fischer). Thus, he led his column of three forward companies head-on towards the two lines of the assembled Lexington militiamen (Fleming).

Major Pitcairn saw what was happening ahead of him and spurred his horse forward in a canter. Unlike Adair, Pitcairn elected to ride to the left around the church. Thus, he lost contact with his men and, more importantly, he lost command control of his forward troops, who marched rapidly out of his sight and

Lexington Green (1712) as it appears today. Every year a re-enactment of the engagement on April 19, 1775 is held here.

beyond his control toward the waiting Lexington militia (Galvin).

Militiamen, straining to see ahead through the dawn darkness, first saw Major Pitcairn appear on horseback on the Concord Road side of the church, followed shortly by three other mounted British officers at full gallop. Militiamen, in depositions sworn just weeks after the battle, testified that they heard the British officers yell conflicting orders: "Disperse ye rebels! Damn you disperse!" (quoted by Jonas Clarke), "Throw down your arms, ye damn rebels!" (testified John Robbins), "Surrender!" "Surround them!" the British officers shouted above the din (Fleming, Fischer, Sawtells, Narrative).

Lexington's Captain Parker immediately turned to his men to give them new orders to comply with the demands of the Britilsh officers. As he later testified, "I immediately ordered our militia to **disperse** and not to fire." Most of the Lexington militiamen consequently turned and started to disperse, walking away from the oncoming British. None, however, laid down their arms. Only two, Jonas Parker and Robert Munroe, remained on the line where they had mustered.

Lieutenant Adair, followed by two companies of Light Infantry, the 4th and the 10th, appeared to the expectant militiamen on the Bedford Road side of the Meeting House, immediately after Major Pitcairn and his fellow mounted officers had appeared on the Concord Road side. On sighting the waiting Lexington militiamen, the Regulars, completely out of contact with their superior officers, lost control and started running haphazardly towards the colonists, bellowing loudly the fierce battle cry of British infantrymen: "Huzzah! Huzzah! Huzzah!"

A shot rang out! Other volleys followed from the muskets of the British Regulars, who then lowered their bayonets and charged into the American ranks. Eight Americans were killed and ten more were wounded. The rest fled through a thick cloud of musket smoke.

Who fired the first shot at Lexington? Over 50 surviving members of Parker's militia, in depositions taken within weeks of the battle, testified that the first gun-fire did not come from *their* ranks (Sawtells, Narrative, Fischer). Many front line British Regulars later swore under oath that it did not come from *their* muskets. Did British Major Pitcairn or Lt. Sutherlund, both on horseback, discharge their pistols first? Did a mysterious Lexington spectator fire from Buckman Tavern, as several witnesses later swore? Did both fire simultaneously? (For excerpts from

Hancock Clarke House (1698)

conflicting eye-witness depositions and accounts by the colonists and by the British, refer to the next section of this book, "Who Fired the First Shot at Lexington?").

Were the first shots fired deliberately or discharged by accident? Unfortunately, we will *never* know with complete certainty who fired the first shot. But we do know that the subsequent fusillade and bayoneting spree by the out-of-control British Regulars was deadly for the Lexington men, causing 18 American casualties.

Jonas Parker, Captain John Parker's cousin, according to orator Edward Everett (1799), "had been often heard to say that 'be the consequences what they might, and let others do what they pleased, but he would never run from the enemy.' He was as good as his word. Having loaded his musket, he placed his hat containing the ammunition on the ground in readiness for a second charge. At the second fire he was wounded and sunk upon his knees; and in this condition discharged his gun. While loading it again on is knees and striving in the agonies of death to redeem his pledge, he was transfixed by a bayonet and thus died on the spot where he first stood and fell" (Edward Everett quoted in Lexington: Birthplace of American Liberty, Lexington Historical Society).

The rest of the slain Lexingtonians were killed, trying to disperse. Jonathan Harrington was mortally wounded only yards from his house across from the Green, as his horrified wife and son watched. Bleeding profusely from a chest wound, he crawled to his front path, and then died on his own doorstep.

While most of the Americans were *dispersing*, only a few American militiamen, like Jonas Parker and John Munroe, both then killed on the spot, managed to discharge their muskets at the charging Regulars. British soldiers testified later that only *one* Regular was actually wounded (in the leg) in the Lexington clash, a Private Thomas Johnson. Ironically, two months later he was mortally wounded at the Battle of Bunker Hill (Fischer).

Revolutionary Sites to Visit Today in Lexington

★ A visitor to the **Lexington Battle Green** (Commons) today will see many reminders of the 1775 conflict. **The Statue of the Lexington Minuteman** stands guard by the entrance to the triangular Green and faces southeast towards Arlington, Cambridge and Boston, the direction

A Patriot Courier is depicted at the Minute Man Visitors' Center on the Lexington/Lincoln line.

from which the British troop columns approached over 200 years ago. Atop a rugged pile of granite boulders, the eight-foot six-inch greenish bronze man stands tall, as tribute to Captain John Parker. "The famous continental soldier is represented in a stern and expectant attitude, bareheaded and in short sleeves prepared to meet his fate in the cause of liberty. The old musket is clasped firmly in both hands, the whole figure representing strength and high purpose" (Boston Globe, 1900, Statue Dedication). H. H. Kitson, a Boston sculptor, crafted the statue in 1900 for the total cost of about $11,000.

The contrast with the other Minuteman statue by Daniel Chester French (1875) in Concord is striking. French's Concord Minuteman carries his musket in his right hand, but his left hand rests on a plow handle, symbolizing clearly that he is a citizen farmer-soldier, not a professional. Of interest is the fact that French's

Buckman Tavern (c.1710).

Concord Minute Man is generally better known. It was used most frequently for patriotic marketing – from World War II War Bonds to U.S. postage stamps and for many logos, such as that of the Sons of the American Revolution (S.A.R.).

★ Also on the Lexington Common, a.k.a. Battle Green, is a **Boulder** with a plaque (D.A.R., 1910) marking the site of the **Old Belfry**, which was originally built in 1761 atop nearby Belfry Hill and then moved down to the Common in 1768 to "hang ye Bell for Town's Use Forever." It stood next to the Meeting House on the Common. The current **reproduction of the Old Belfry** was rebuilt in 1910 and stands again atop **Belfry Hill**, off Massachusetts Avenue and Clarke Street.

★ The granite obelisk **Revolutionary Battle Monument** on the west side of the Common was erected in 1799 in memory of the Lexington men who fought and died here in 1775. In 1835 the remains of the slain Lexington Minute Men were transferred from a common grave at the Old Burying Ground and deposited in a

The famous "Doolittle Prints" are the closest that we will ever come to a graphic depiction of the events of April 19, 1775, created close in time of the actual events. They were drawn several weeks after the battles by Ralph Earle, a Connecticut militiaman, who was stationed in Cambridge. He traveled to Concord, sketched the battle sites and interviewed eye-witnesses. Earle's drawings were then engraved by Amos Doolittle of New Haven. First published in 1775, they are reputed to be the first series of historical prints ever published in the United States. The originals are owned by the Connecticut Historical Society in Hartford. The Battle of Lexington, April 19th, 1775 depicts the 5 A.M. encounter between the invading expeditionary force of about 700 British Regulars, led by Lt. Col. Francis Smith and Major John Pitcairn, and 77 Lexington militiamen, led by Captain John Parker. This scene was sketched by Ralph Earle and engraved by Amos Doolittle.

tomb to the rear of the Monument.

The 1799 inscription by the Rev. Jonas Clarke lists the names of the slain men and asserts the Monument is "Sacred to Liberty & The Rights of Mankind!!! The Freedom of Independence of America Sealed and Defended with the Blood of her Sons. The First Victims To The Sword of British Tyranny & Oppression. They rose as One Man to Revenge Their Brethren's Blood, And Defend Their Native Rights. They Nobly Dar'D to Be Free!!!"

★ The **Lexington Revolutionary Battle Monument** has witnessed much more history. Beside it, French Marquis de Lafayette, hero of both the American and French Revolutions, was welcomed to Lexington in 1824; the Centennial was celebrated (with Concord) in 1875; WW I soldiers were bid farewell in 1917 and welcomed home again in 1919; townspeople pledged themselves to fight for liberty in WW II in 1942; and in the 1975 Bicentennial thousands rededicated the Common and reaffirmed their belief in democracy. Ceremonies are held beside the Monument each April on Patriots' Day.

★ The Lexington Historical Society owns and operates **Buckman Tavern, The Hancock-Clarke House** and the **Munroe Tavern**. Experienced guides conduct tours during regularly scheduled hours and each house has its own Gift Shop. An

entry fee is charged for each house.

★ **Buckman Tavern** was the rendezvous spot of the Lexington Minuteman. They quaffed flip and grog between the moment they were dismissed by Captain John Parker at about 1:30 am, April 19, 1775 and when they responded to William Diamond's drum roll by remustering on the Common at about 4:30 am, just prior to the appearance of the Regulars.

Visitors enter the restored Tap Room with its great fireplace. Long muskets hang on the walls and antique jugs, flip mugs, bottles and loggerheads (heating irons) adorn the shelves. A costumed guide shows guests the Kitchen, Ladies' Parlor and Landlord's Bedroom – all furnished with authentic antiques.

★ **The Hancock-Clarke House**, one block from the Common on 36 Hancock Street, was built in about 1698. It was the long time home for the families of ministers Rev. John Hancock (for 54 years) and Rev. Jonas Clarke (50 years). Early on the morning of April 19, 1775 the arrival of first Paul Revere and then William Dawes roused Samuel Adams and John Hancock, the minister's grandson, and a Signer of the Declaration of Independence. They were staying there as representatives to the Second Provincial Congress in Concord. Forewarned of the imminent approach of the British, the two Patriots were transported by coach to Woburn, then to Billerica, four miles away, where they joined Hancock's

The Belfry (1761) stood in Lexington during the Revolution adjacent to the Church on the Common (no longing standing). When the bell in this tower sounded the alarm early on April 19, 1775, it summoned militia and Minutemen from as far as three miles away. The original belfry was destroyed by a gale in 1900; this replica was built on a nearby rise in 1910.

betrothed, Dorothy Quincy, for a repast of "cold salt pork and potatoes."

★ **Munroe Tavern** at 1332 Massachusetts Avenue, a mile east of the Battle Green, is also open to the public in season. Built in 1695, it was bought by Sergeant William Munroe in 1770. On the afternoon of April 19, 1775 General Hugh, Lord Percy's British relief brigade marched westward from Boston to Lexington with over 1,000 reinforcements to relieve Lieutenant Colonel Francis Smith's embattled troops, who were fleeing eastward from Concord. Percy made the old hostelry his headquarters. Wounded Regulars were tended to. Exhausted Redcoats rested and refreshed themselves at the Tavern's expense. The British wantonly shot and killed John Raymond, a crippled man whom Sergeant Munroe had left in charge of his tavern. (The bullet hole remains in the bar room ceiling). Besides the Tap Room, visitors can see relics of George Washington's visit to the Tavern in 1789, as well as authentic period furniture, such as a four-poster bed and spinning wheels.

★ **The Museum of Our National Heritage**, on Route 2A and Marrett Road, has changing exhibits about American history and culture and an ongoing exhibit, "Lexington Alarm'd!," which explores causes and consequences of the American Revolution. The Museum and its library were built and are operated by the Scottish Rite Masonic Order and have permanent exhibits about the history of American fraternal orders, such as the Masons, to which many American Revolutionary officers and soldiers belonged. Entry is free.

★ **Minute Man National Historical Park** encompasses historic structures and landscapes in Lexington, Lincoln and Concord along the Battle Road, paralleling Route 2A. Mindful of the approaching Bicentennial, President Eisenhower signed the law creating the Park in 1959 and it was dedicated in 1976. Currently over one

★ LEXINGTON ★

A detail of A View of the South Part of Lexington depicts the British retreat or "running skirmish" along the Battle Road at about 4 PM. on April 19, 1775. The British brigade of about 700 Regulars (right) is retreating from Concord. They are met by a relief column of about 1000 fresh British reinforcements (left), led by General Hugh Percy who meets with Lt. Col. Francis Smith (center). Colonial militia and Minutemen from many neighboring towns fire their muskets at the Redcoats from the protection of stone wall and trees. British artillery men aim a cannon at the Lexington Meeting House. Flames and smoke rise from Lexington Houses that have been torched by the retreating British troops. Ralph Earle was the artist and Amos Doolittle the engraver.

million people visit the Park each year.

According to Lawrence D. Gall, former Park Superintendent, the stated objective of managing the land in Lexington, Lincoln and Concord, which comprises the Park as a "living cultural landscape" is to help visitors understand "changes brought on by human use and to interpret land use patterns to place the events of April 19, 1775 in their historical context by giving Park visitors a better understanding of a society whose members felt compelled to resist British authority" (French).

Sources:

Most of the historical references referred to in this chapter about the Battle of Lexington Green are listed in detail under Sources after the chapter about the Concord Fight, on page 74.

Other References, covering primarily the Battle of Lexington, include:
Chamberlain, Samuel, Lexington and Concord, Hastings House, 1988 (photos).
Lexington Historical Society, Lexington: Birthplace of American Liberty, 1995.
Lexington Historical Society, Three Lexington Landmarks, 1998.
Sideris, Lou (Chief of Interpretation, Minute Man National Historical Park, Lexington and Concord, MA.), Personal communication, 1999.
Sileo, Thomas P., History of the Lexington Battlegreen, Acton, 1995.
Sterzin, Emily, Lexington Battlegreen: A Walking Guide, Lexington Historical Society, 1998.
Tourtellot, A., Lexington and Concord: The Beginning of the War of the American Revolution (originally published as: William Diamond's Drum), Norton, 1959.

★ ★ ★ ★

Who Fired the First Shot at Lexington?
Depositions of People Who Were There

*These conflicting sworn eye-witness accounts were given by both invading British soldiers and defending Lexington militia. Who **did** fire the first shot? Whom do you believe? Perhaps we will **never** know with certainty. This presentation was inspired by a permanent exhibit at the Museum of Our Natural Heritage in Lexington, "Let It Begin Here! Lexington and the Revolution."*

What the Patriots Said

★ "Whilst our backs were turned on the troops, we were fired on by them, and a number of our men were instantly killed and wounded, not a gun was fired by any person in our company on the regulars before they fired on us…"
—Collective deposition of 34 Lexington Minutemen, April 25, 1775.

★ "I heard one of the regulars, whom I took to be an officer, say, damn them we will have them, and immediately the regulars shouted aloud, run and fired on the Lexington Company, which did not fire a gun before the regulars discharged them…"
—Elijah Sanderson, Lexington bystander, deposition, April 19, 1775.

★ "(I) ordered our militia to meet on the common in said Lexington, to consult what to do, and concluded not to be discovered nor meddle or make with said regular troops (if they should approach) unless they should insult or molest us, and upon their sudden approach, I immediately ordered our militia to disperse and not to fire. Immediately said troops made their appearance and rushing furiously, fired upon and killed eight of our party, without receiving any provocation therefore from us."
—Captain John Parker, Lexington Minutemen, deposition, April 25, 1775.

★ "The Second of (the British) officers fired a pistol towards the militia, as they were dispersing."
—Rev. Jonas Clarke

★ "(T)he commanding officer of (the British) troops, as I took him, gave the command to the troops 'fire! fire! damn you fire!' and immediately they fired, before any of Captain Parker's company fired."
—William Draper, Middlesex Militiamen, April 25, 1775.

What the British Said

★ "(O)n our coming near (the rebels) they fired one or two shots, upon which our Men without any orders rushed in upon them, fired and put'em to flight."
–Lt. John Barker, 4th Regiment, Eyewitness Account from his diary, The British in Boston.

★ "Some of the rebels who jumped over the wall, fired four or five shott at the soldiers."
–Major John Pitcairn, British Marines.

★ "3 shot were fired from a corner of a large house to the right of the Church."
–Lieutenant William Sutherland, 38th Regiment in a letter to Sir Henry Clinton, April 26, 1775.

★ "(W)hen one of the rebels fired a shot, our soldiers returned the fire and killed about fourteen of them."
–Ensign De Berniere's Account Report to General Gage on April 19, 1775.

★ "Which party fired first I cannot exactly say."
–Lt. Edward Gould, 4th Regiment, April 25, 1775.

Sources:
Force, Peter, American Archives: A Documentary History, Volume II, *Washington, 1839.*
Fischer, David H., Paul Revere's Ride, *1994.*
Kehoe, Vincent, We Were There!, *1994.*
Sawtell, Clement, The Nineteeth of April, 1775: A Collection of First Hand Accounts, *Lincoln, Ma., 1968.*
Soldiers, American, A Narrative of the Excursion and Ravages of the King's Troops with Depositions, Watertown, MA, May 22, 1775 *(Reprinted by the New England & Virginia Company).*

★ ★ ★ ★

An Hour By Hour Chronicle of Two Fateful April Days in 1775

TUESDAY, APRIL 18, 1775

10:00 P.M. **Boston** — On the orders of the British Governor, General Thomas Gage, about 700 Grenadiers and Light Infantry are awakened to carry out a secret march to Concord to search for and destroy hidden Colonial weapons and supplies.

10:30 P.M. Boston — Dr. Joseph Warren alerts William Dawes, Jr. and Paul Revere about British troop movement.

— Dawes is dispatched on horse by land over the Boston Neck to Lexington.

— Revere has two lanterns hung in the steeple of the Old North Church by Sexton Robert Newman to notify Patriots in Charlestown that the British will travel "by sea,"i.e. across the river.

— British troops assemble on Boston Common, then embark by boats across the Back Bay of the Charles River to Cambridge.

11:00 P.M. Charlestown — Revere arrives, after being rowed across the Charles River. He leaves by horse and gallops towards Lexington to spread the alarm.

Map of Minute Man National Historical Park in Lexington, Lincoln and Concord Massachussets. The Park preserves land around the original 1775 Battle Road, the route of British troops, who marched westward from Boston to Concord on April 19, 1775 to seize weapons hidden by dissident colonists. After fighting battles with the colonists on the Lexington Green and at the North Bridge in Concord, British Redcoats retreated from Concord back to Boston along the same route, but now pursued by thousands of colonial militia and Minutemen, with whom they fought fierce battles in the so-called "running skirmish." Modern Route 2A runs through the Park, which includes the Minute Man Visitors' Center on the Lexington/Lincoln line, the Battle Road Trail for walking and biking (dotted lines), and the North Bridge Visitors' Center and the Wayside in Concord.

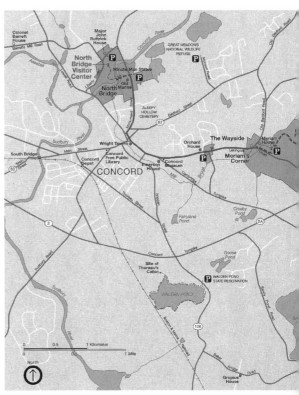

★ CHRONOLOGY OF APRIL 18 & 19, 1775 ★

WEDNESDAY, APRIL 19, 1775

Midnight Lexington — Revere arrives at the Parson Jonas Clarke's House.

12:30 A.M. Lexington — Dawes arrives at the Hancock-Clarke House.

— The Belfry Bell on the Lexington Green is rung and about 130 Minute Men, under Capt. John Parker, assemble on the Green.

— Dr. Samuel Prescott of Concord joins Revere and Dawes as they ride westward.

1:00 A.M. Lincoln — British officers on an advance patrol capture Revere. Dawes escapes to Lexington.

— Prescott jumps over a stone wall and escapes, then gallops westward to Concord.

2:00 A.M. Concord — Prescott arrives; the Town House bell is rung. Three companies of Concord Minutemen gather at Wright's Tavern.

Cambridge — British troops begin the march from Cambridge to Lexington.

2:30 A.M. Lincoln — Revere is released by British, returns on foot to **Lexington** to warn John Hancock and Samuel Adams to leave the Hancock-Clarke House. They depart.

4:30 A.M. Lexington — A scout reports the British Regulars are near, the drum is beat and 77 Minutemen muster, then line up in a double row on Lexington Green.

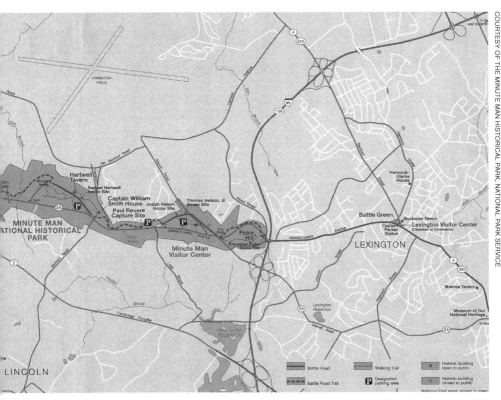

★ CHRONOLOGY OF APRIL 18 & 19, 1775 ★

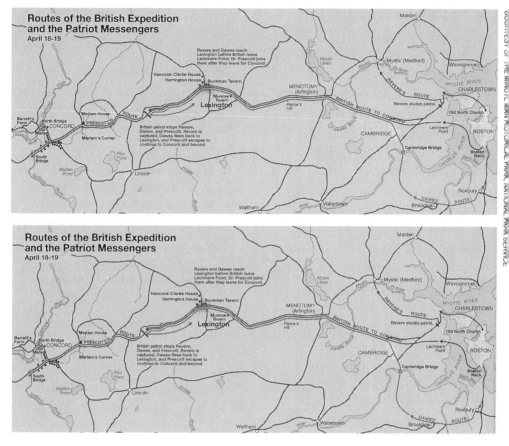

5:00 A.M. Lexington — Major John Pitcairn's Redcoats face Captain John Parker's Minutemen. A single shot rings out! Then a volley from the British platoon. Eight Americans are killed and ten wounded. The first American blood has been shed!

5:30 A.M. Lexington — British Regulars march towards Concord.

7:00 A.M. Concord — British troops arrive in Concord Center. Minutemen withdraw.

7:30 A.M. Concord — Lt. Colonel Francis Smith orders three British companies to guard the North Bridge, four companies to march to Colonel James Barrett's farm to search for hidden weapons, and one company to hold the South Bridge.

8:00 A.M. Concord — The Minutemen withdraw to Punkatasset Hill, as the Redcoats arrive at the North Bridge, and two British companies cross over the bridge to the west bank of the Concord River.

8:30 A.M. Concord — British Grenadiers inadvertently set fire to the Town House in Concord Center, when they are burning wooden gun carriages.

9:00 A.M. Concord — The Minutemen see the smoke and believe the British are torching Concord deliberately. The Colonials march toward the North Bridge.

— Joseph Hosmer of Concord asks, "Will you let them burn the town down?"

— The British retreat over the bridge to the east bank of the Concord River.

9:30 A.M. Concord — The Redcoats open fire across the North Bridge and kill two Minutemen, Captain Isaac Davis and Abner Hosmer, both from Acton.

— Major John Buttrick of Concord then shouts, "Fire, fellow soldiers, for God's sake, fire!"

— The Minutemen advance and fire.

— Three British privates are killed and four officers wounded.

— The British abruptly turn and flee towards Concord Center.

10:00 A.M. Concord — The British troops reassemble in Concord Center at Wright's Tavern to rest and eat.

12:00 NOON Concord — British troops leave Concord to march eastward towards Boston.

12:30 P.M. Concord — At Meriam's Corner over 1,000 militia from neighboring towns fire on and pursue the retreating Redcoats. The "running skirmish" (or "ambush") has begun.

1:30 P.M. Lincoln — The Americans, firing from behind cover of walls and trees, kill many British soldiers at the "Bloody Angle."

2:00 P.M. Lexington — Captain John Parker's Minutemen get their revenge by firing from a hill at the retreating Redcoats.

3:00 P.M. Lexington — British General Hugh Percy, having marched from Boston with 1,000 fresh Redcoat reinforcements, relieves Colonel Smith's exhausted Redcoats and fires cannons to slow the advancing Americans. Percy's and Smith's Regulars rest at Munroe Tavern.

5:30 P.M. Arlington (Menotomy) — Fierce fighting between the retreating Redcoats and the pursuing Minutemen. Many killed.

7:00 P.M. Charlestown Neck — Exhausted British troops, having marched over 40 miles in 21 hours with no sleep and little food or water and having been under constant hostile fire for over 8 hours, stagger into Charlestown.

10:00 P.M. Boston — Wounded British troops are ferried back to Boston.

PAST MIDNIGHT — Other British troops return to Boston by boat.

THE TALLY —73 British soldiers are killed, 174 wounded, and 26 missing. 49 Americans are killed, 41 are wounded, and 5 are missing.

★ *The Revolution has begun! It would require eight more years of fierce battles to conclude, with the American victory at Yorktown, VA, in 1781 and the Peace Treaty in Paris in 1783, granting America independence from England.*

— J.L.A.

Source: Concord Chamber of Commerce, Lexington–Concord Battle Road: Hour By Hour Account of April 19, 1775.

★ ★ ★ ★

Battle Road near the Concord/Lincoln line as seen in a historic 1880's photograph by Concord photographer, Alfred Hosmer.

★ ★ ★ ★

New Developments at Minute Man Park and the New Battle Road Trail

BY LOU SIDERIS

inute Man National Historical Park in Lexington, Lincoln and Concord has recently seen exciting new developments that will greatly enhance future visits to the Park, increase understanding of the Park's story, and strengthen connections between the Park and local communities.

The Park's **Minute Man Visitor Center** (formally called Battle Road Visitor Center), on Route 2A at the Lincoln/Lexington town line has been completely renovated with all new exhibits. One feature of the exhibit design is a specially commissioned 40 foot mural by artist John Rush that depicts Colonists and British Redcoats fighting along the Battle Road (which graces this book's cover).

★ The Minute Man Visitors Center also features a new **multimedia theater program, "The Road to Revolution."** This program, in one of the Center's two theaters, educates visitors about the events of April 18-19, 1775 by the use of movie and video screens, sequenced lighting of historic displays, an electric map of the Battle Road and surround- sound. All these modern media help to tell the

Minute Man Visitors' Center on the Lexington/Lincoln line near Battle Road.

story of Paul Revere's ride from Boston and the battles of Lexington and Concord. This exciting show is free.

★ The **Battle Road Trail,** a new 5.5 mile historic trail, connects points of interest in the Park. This new trail and its associated facilities (parking lots, restrooms, markers, and signage) greatly enhances the way visitors access and enjoy the park.

The main theme of the trail is the Battle of April 19, 1775, that launched the American Revolution. In addition, the trail allows interpretation of natural history and the broader "human story." It tells the story of the people whose lives were altered by the events that took place here.

Much of the trail follows original remnants of the Battle Road. Trail construction funding enabled the Park to remove modern asphalt and restore several sections of this historic "highway." Other trail sections leave the historic road to follow the route of the Minutemen, traversing farming fields, wetlands, and forests. Before now, the diverse resources of the **Battle Road Unit** of the park have been mostly unknown and inaccessible to visitors.

Park visitors are now able to walk, bicycle, or use a wheelchair to enjoy the entire 5.5 mile trail, or to visit portions of it. Secondary trails in many areas allow walkers to loop back to the main trail.

Because the **Battle Road Trail** is primarily an educational trail, it is not suitable for high speed bicycling, and the loose stone dust surface will not allow for rollerblading. Bicycles share the trail with pedestrians, wheelchairs, and children in strollers.

Granite obelisks mark the historic **Battle Road**, and low granite markers highlight the locations of historic houses. Locations of **gravesites**, where fallen British Redcoats were buried by local townspeople after the battle are marked.

★ The **Paul Revere Capture Site** in Lincoln (where a ceremony by the Lincoln Minutemen is performed each Patriot's Day weekend) was re-landscaped and enhanced. Historic landscape rehabilitation, including clearing of farm fields and enhancement of vistas, was achieved in many areas.

As a global symbol of man's universal struggle for liberty, Minute Man National Historical Park attracts about one million visitors each year from all over the world. These exciting new improvements will help enable the Park to more effectively fulfill its promise.

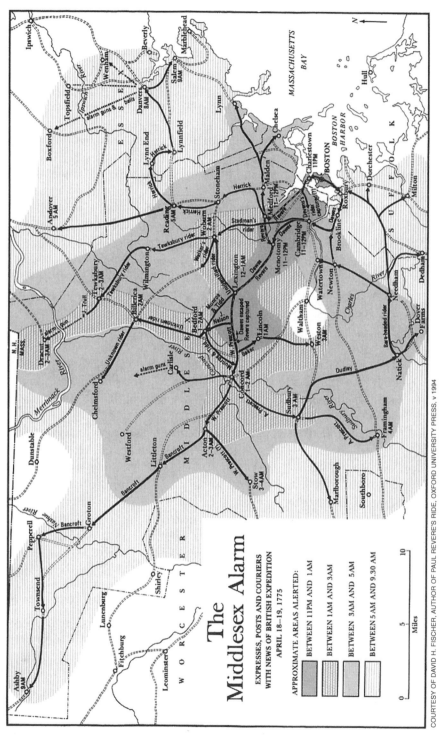

The
Middlesex Alarm

EXPRESSES, POSTS AND COURIERS
WITH NEWS OF BRITISH EXPEDITION
APRIL 18—19, 1775

APPROXIMATE AREAS ALERTED:

BETWEEN 11PM AND 1AM

BETWEEN 1AM AND 3AM

BETWEEN 3AM AND 5AM

BETWEEN 5AM AND 9.30 AM

COURTESY OF DAVID H. FISCHER, AUTHOR OF PAUL REVERE'S RIDE, OXFORD UNIVERSITY PRESS, v 1994

Outline of East Coast, Lexington and Concord Settlements

-10,000 B.C.E. Native Americans, Algonquians, live along the East Coast and inland.

1585 English colonists, sent by Sir Walter Raleigh, start their first American settlement on **Roanoke Island**, N.C. (Elizabeth I is Queen of England).

1607 **Jamestown,** Virginia, is founded after a charter from King James I.

1620 Pilgrims end 3-month voyage on the **Mayflower**, reach Cape Cod, found colony at **Plymouth**, Massachusetts.

1630 **Boston, Massachusetts** is founded by John Winthrop and members of Massachusetts Bay Colony. Puritans begin "Great Migration" from England to Massachusetts and Connecticut.

1635 **Concord** is founded at the site of a Native American village, **Musketaquid** ("Reedy River"). A town petition to the Massachusetts General Court is granted to Simon Willard, a merchant from Kent, who arrived in Boston in 1634 and traded furs with Indians west of Boston. Concord is the first inland town west of the sea coast. Rev. Peter Bulkely, Rev. John Jones and carpenter Thomas Dane move to Concord.

1636 English settlers purchase "six myles square" in a "concord" (agreement) with Squaw Sachem and her tribe of Algonquian Indians.

1642 Benjamin Muzzey builds a house and clears land in **Cambridge Farms**, site of today's Lexington.

1675 **King Phillips War**, Massasoit's son attacks Colonial settlements, is then defeated.

1685 **King James II revokes the Massachusetts Charter** and appoints a Governor, Edmund Andros. Land titles are voided, town meetings lose their rights to tax, Episcopal churches established.

1689 After James II flees to France, Concord and other **towns' militias march to Boston** and arrest Governor Andros. William and Mary come to power, issue **new Massachusetts Charter**, restoring land rights and taxation by towns.

1713 **Lexington**, named after Robert Sutton, Lord Lexington, is incorporated.

★ ★ ★ ★

Lincoln: Battle Road Runs Through It

BY DONALD L. HAFNER

he Town of Lincoln lying between Lexington and Concord, contains a long segment of the original **Battle Road**, restored (as much as modern conditions permit) to its appearance in 1775.

In the 1770s, Lincoln was a farming community of only 750 residents, a few of whom were Tories, but most were Patriots. As political tensions with the British government grew, the voters of Lincoln agreed in January 1775 to raise a company of Minutemen, at the urging of the Massachusetts Provincial Congress. Yet in true Yankee fashion, the town did not vote to pay for them until three months later on March 20th:

"Voted as followes that the Sum of fifty-two Pounds four Shillings be and is hereby granted to provide for those persons who have inlisted as minute men each one a bayonet belt Catrige Box Steal ramer gun stock and knap sack; they to attend military Exercise four hours in a day twice in a week … the officers to keep an exact account of their attendance" (MacLean, 254).

Under colonial laws dating to the 1600s, all males between the ages of 16 and 45 were required to be members of the militia, and Lincoln had a regular militia company. The wisdom of preparing a portion of the militia to march "at a moment's notice," as well as the name "Minutemen," were also old ideas, and Lincoln's elder veterans from The French and Indian War knew what was required. The town raised a company of sixty-two Minutemen, the majority of them young and sturdy farmers' sons, unmarried and living with their parents. They elected William Smith

Hartwell Tavern. Originally home to Ephraim and Elizabeth Hartwell and their children it also served as a tavern and stopping place for travelers and drovers on the way to and from Boston. Restored by the National Park Service as part of Minute Man National Historic Park, it now hosts visitors on tours by historic interpreters.

as their captain. He was only 29 years old, and he had no battlefield experience. (Many of Lincoln's older community leaders had already accepted higher positions in the Massachusetts militia.) But Smith was one of the largest property holders in town — and he was the brother-in-law of John Adams, the Patriot leader and future President.

In Lincoln, the events of April 19th began with Paul Revere's capture and an uncommon act of bravery by Mary Flint Hartwell, wife of a sergeant of the Lincoln Minutemen. When Revere and his companions, William Dawes and Dr. Samuel Prescott, were intercepted in Lincoln by a British patrol at about one o'clock in the morning while attempting to carry the alarm to Concord, Prescott escaped by galloping his horse through a neighboring swamp. When he returned to the road further on and awakened the Hartwell house, Samuel Hartwell made ready to join his Minuteman unit while Mary walked into the night — and toward the British patrol — to carry the alarm to their neighbor, Captain William Smith. Smith rode to the town center, rang the meeting house bell, and ordered the Lincoln Minutemen to head for Concord. Soon Minutemen and militia members converged on Lincoln's country roads and marched in defense of American liberty. Decades later, Amos Baker, a private in Lincoln's militia and the last surviving participant in the battle at the North Bridge, would recall the scene: "When I went to Concord in the morning, I joined the Lincoln company at the brook, by Flint's pond... I loaded my gun there with two balls, ounce (sic) balls, and powder accordingly." The Lincoln Minutemen and militia were the first units to reach Concord that April morning.

An incident at the North Bridge involving a Lincoln militia man reminds us how divided communities were over the dispute with Great Britain. James Nichols was an English immigrant and a farmer in Lincoln, well liked as "a good droll fellow and a fine singer." But as he watched the Redcoats assembled at the bridge, he suddenly said to the men standing near him, "If any of you will hold my gun, I will go down and talk with them." He walked over to the British soldiers, spoke with them briefly, then returned to his militia company, retrieved his musket and announced that he was going home (Fischer, 209). How well James Nichols fared afterward in the small town of Lincoln we can only guess. Later, his neighbors accepted him back into the Lincoln militia, which was then helping lay siege to the British in Boston. But not long after, Nichols deserted to the British side and was not heard from again.

★ A stone monument and plaque at the Paul Revere Capture Site (1775) mark the approximate place where these historic events began. All that survives of the **Samuel and Mary Flint Hartwell House** which was almost destroyed by a fire in later years, is the cellar and an elaborate chimney studded with fireplaces, but they give visitors a unique opportunity to view the sturdy backbone of a typical New England colonial house. Nearby, the **William Smith House (1693)** and the **Hartwell Tavern**, which was run by Samuel's father, have been restored by the Minute Man National Park and are open to visitors and staffed by historical interpreters.

William Smith House, along the Battle Road in Lincoln.

★ The segment of the **Battle Road** that runs through Lincoln is only two and a half miles long. Yet so intense was the fighting along this stretch that the retreating British soldiers nearly exhausted their ammunition and their discipline. The skirmishes at Lexington Green (at 5 AM) and Concord's North Bridge (at 9:30 AM) had produced deaths and great anger on both sides, but they had not yet provoked a sustained battle. All that would change in Lincoln.

★ In early afternoon, just to the west of town, at **Meriam's Corner in Concord**, the militias gathering from towns near and far now outnumbered the Redcoats, and they began to form in battle lines. As the British column marched past on its return eastward to Boston, a sharp exchange of musket fire occurred, and several British soldiers fell, dead and wounded. The Redcoats tried to move more briskly as they crossed into Lincoln, but again and again the Americans formed deadly ambushes in the woods and behind the piled stone walls that lined the road—at **Brook's Hill**, at the curves in the road now called **Bloody Angle**, and around the barn and buildings of Samuel and Mary Hartwell's farm. The Americans aimed especially at the British officers, creating great disorder among the troops. And further to the east, at the Lexington boundary, Minutemen from Lincoln joined with Captain John Parker's men of Lexington in yet another ambush, this one in revenge for the killings on Lexington Green that morning. As it left Lincoln, the British column was disintegrating into a running mob, pursued now by several thousand Americans.

Given the great terror inflicted on the Redcoats in Lincoln on April 19th, it is fitting that the day was followed by a noble act of compassion—by Mary Hartwell. Ten British soldiers were killed along the Battle Road in Lincoln, eight of them within yards of the Hartwell home. The morning after the battle, as Mary Hartwell later recounted:

Battle Road intepretive trail in Lincoln.

"The men hitched the oxen to the cart and gathered up the dead. As they returned with the team and the dead soldiers, my thoughts went out for the wives, parents, and children across the Atlantic, who would never again see their loved ones; and I left the house, and taking my little children by the hand, I followed the rude hearse to the grave hastily made in the burial ground. I remember how cruel it seemed to put them into one large trench without any coffins. There was one in a brilliant uniform, whom I supposed to have been an officer" (MacLean, 282).

★ In 1884, the citizens of Lincoln placed a memorial stone over the **British Gravesite** in the **old town cemetery on Lexington Road in Lincoln**. Each April, to the sound of muffled drums, fifes, and bagpipe, the modern Lincoln Minutemen assemble with Redcoat units to commemorate the sacrifices of these soldiers and of the Lincoln Revolutionary heroes (including Mary Hartwell) who are buried nearby. Visitors to the old town cemetery will find the graves marked by small flags.

★ The original **Lincoln Town Center**, at the intersection of Trapelo and Bedford Roads, retains much of the charm of a New England farm community, with houses and buildings dating to the 1700s and early-1800s clustered around a white church built in the traditional style. All that remains of the original meeting house where Captain Smith rang the alarm is an **old graveyard**, where the stones bear the names of many of Lincoln's Revolutionary soldiers. Standing amidst these graves and gazing northward in the direction of the **Battle Road**, past the houses and barns and open fields, a visitor with a lively imagination might still hear the fife and drum and the crackle of musket fire — and the birth of American Independence.

Sources:

MacLean, John C., *A Rich Harvest: The History, Buildings, and People of Lincoln, Massachusetts*, Lincoln Historical Society, 1987.

Hersey, Frank W., *Heroes of the Battle Road*, Perry Walton, 1930.

Brooks, Paul, *The View from Lincoln Hill*, Houghton Mifflin, 1976.

Fischer, David Hackett, *Paul Revere's Ride*, Oxford, 1994.

★ ★ ★ ★

Concord: "The Shot Heard 'Round the World!"

A visitor to Concord on a pilgrimage to trace America's Revolutionary roots might best start at the **North Bridge**. This arched wooden span over the gently flowing Concord River was the site of the second interchange of gunshots between King George III's British Redcoats and the Colonial farmer-soldiers on April 19, 1775.

Colonists and British Regulars had exchanged musket fire earlier that morning on the Lexington Green, but there Captain Parker's Lexington militiamen were "dispersing," pursued by Redcoats. However, the Concord Fight at the North Bridge represented, as the inscription carved into the marble of Concord's 1836 **Battle Monument** states, the first American "forcible resistance" to British imperial troops (Ripley, French).

The fact that this bloody fire fight between colonial militiamen and troops of their British overlords occurred at this **North Bridge** on the Concord River location seems incongruous in light of the scene today's visitor sees here: a tranquil green setting of field, forest, meadow, and stream.

The Concord Minuteman Statue (1875) by Daniel Chester French was commissioned for the Centennial of the Concord Fight. Here it is visited by tourist pilgrims of the late 19th variety.

★ CONCORD ★

April 19, 1775 In Concord

Concord's Dr. Samuel Prescott galloped from Lexington into **Concord Center** at 2 a.m. to spread the alarm that 700 British Regulars had left Boston and indeed were marching towards Lexington and Concord, presumably to search for, seize and destroy hidden American arms caches in Concord. Immediately after Dr. Prescott's arrival in Concord, the Town House bell was rung to alert Concord's militia and Minutemen to assemble immediately. Three companies of Concord Minutemen left their houses to gather at **Wright Tavern** (1747).

They talked with their minister, Rev. William Emerson (grandfather of Ralph Waldo Emerson), and agreed to send several "posts" (scouts) to gallop down the Bay Road towards Lexington to reconnoiter and get more detailed information about the advancing British forces. One "post," Reuben Brown, a harness and saddle maker, reached the Lexington Green just as the Regulars were arriving. As the firing began, he turned his horse and galloped back to Concord, without learning the details of the battle. When questioned by Major John Buttrick as to whether the Regulars were actually firing musket balls (not just exploding powder), he replied, "I do not know, but think it probably." Thus, the fearful Concord farmer-soldiers did not know for certain, as they waited whether the British troops, about to invade their village, were merely trying to scare them by firing blanks or to kill them.

The Minutemen at **Wright Tavern** agreed that they should defend themselves, but not fire first. They marched eastward and about a mile from town first spotted the frightening sight of a long column of about 700 Redcoats advancing rapidly with muskets and bayonets "glistening" in the rising sun. They withdrew to a hill above the Meeting House. Rev. Emerson urged on this troops: "Let us stand our ground. If we die, let us die heroes."

As the larger British forces continued their advance, the Concordians agreed they should execute a strategic retreat. Colonel Barrett led them across the **North Bridge** to regroup on **Punkatasset Hill**, about a mile northwest of Concord Center.

After the British regiments arrived in **Concord Center**, British Lieutenant Colonel Smith and Major Pitcairn surveyed the town through a spy glass from the **Old Hill Burying Ground**. Then they sent their troops in several directions. One company marched out from the village center to secure the **South Bridge** over the Sudbury River to the east. Four companies marched westward two miles to Colonel Barrett's farm and mill, where Tory spies had previously reported that the Minutemen had hidden their supplies. Since Paul Revere's April 7 warning ride to Concord, most of the military supplies had been already moved from Colonel Barrett's farm to neighboring towns. Just before the Regulars reached **Colonel Barrett's farm**, his sons plowed the fields and hid the remaining weapons underground in soil of fresh furrows.

The British search party entered Colonel Barrett's house, and finding nothing suspicious, went to the attic, "where the ammunition was actually hidden, under

First Parish Church (190l) on Lexington Road is on the site of Concord's Third Meeting House Church (1711), where the defiant Massachusetts First Provincial Congress met in 1774. In this photo it is viewed from the **Old Hill Burying Ground** (1600's), which is across the street.

feathers for Mrs. Barrett's feather bed. She thrust her hands into the feathers, and, giving them a flip, filled the air with down. The soldiers were so busy brushing the feathers from their fine uniforms that they searched no further" (Fenn).

Concord men were now reinforced by Minutemen and militiamen, who marched from Acton, Lincoln, Bedford, Carlisle, Westford, Chelmsford, Littleton, Stow and Groton, and other nearby towns from the west and north. (Before the day was over twenty-seven Massachusetts towns would provide militia and/or Minutemen for the fights at Lexington and Concord, as detailed on the table on page 104). Now a force of about 400, they descended from Punkatasset Hill and advanced to the **muster field** directly above the **North Bridge**. The British soldiers retreated down the hill and crossed the North Bridge to the east bank of the Concord River. Next, the Americans formed a long line facing the bridge.

Meanwhile Colonel Smith and Major Pitcairn led British Grenadiers into the now almost deserted **Concord Center**, where they systematically (without warrants) searched suspicious houses for weapons. They searched the house of Lieutenant Joseph Hosmer, a cabinet maker and leader of the more rebellious younger Concord men, who often argued against their most cautious elders. "They did not, however, discover the supply of ammunition, because it was hidden beneath Hosmer's aged mother, as she lay in her feather bed. The family silver was tied to a rope and lowered into the well" (Fenn).

The British searchers did uncover three buried cannons, which they discovered by extracting the secret location from Whig tavern keeper Ephraim Jones. This

The Old Manse (c. 1770), on Monument Street in Concord overlooks the Concord River and the North Bridge. Originally home to minister Rev. William Emerson, it is where his grandson Ralph Waldo Emerson wrote his most famous essays and for several years served as the honeymoon house for author Nathaniel Hawthorne and his bride. As an historic house, it is a gem to visit, since it still houses many of its original furnishings.

was accomplished when Major Pitcairn held a pistol to Jones' head and threatened to use it. Under these circumstances Jones did talk and reluctantly revealed the once secret hiding place for the munitions.

In a symbolic act to punish the defiant colonists, the British soldiers chopped down the Concord liberty pole and burned it.

British troops then set fire to some wooden gun carriages. The flames spread to the **Town House** and set its roof ablaze. An elderly Concord lady pleaded with the Regulars to help douse the flames. Then Colonists and their British invaders momentarily forged a practical temporary alliance. Together they formed a bucket brigade, extinguished the fire and saved the building.

However, smoke from the burning roof, which billowed high above the village, conveyed a message which was to be misinterpreted by both the Colonial and British soldiers facing each other a half mile away at the North Bridge. Both the American farmer-soldiers on the hill and the British Regulars at the North Bridge believed that the smoke they saw rising above Concord Center signified that the British company in the village was deliberately, not inadvertently, torching the buildings of Concord Center.

The colonists were enraged by what they interpreted as the malicious intent of the Redcoats to destroy their village. Lieutenant Joseph Hosmer challenged the cautious restraint of his superior officer, Colonel Barrett, by asking provocatively, "Will you let them burn the town down?" Colonel Barret acquiesced to his mens' anger.

The Americans quickly prepared for action. Captain Isaac Davis of Acton, drew his sword, and, asked by Colonel Barret if he as ready to fight, replied, "I haven't a man who is afraid to go!" Colonel Barrett ordered his men to place shot in their muskets. He still insisted that his men not fire first, but only return fire if the

Regulars fired first. Thus, as historian David H. Fischer points out, the strategies of the American officers at the Lexington Green at 5 a.m. and those at the North Bridge at 9:30 a.m. actually "were remarkably similar, to challenge the British force, but **not** to fire the first shot."

The Provincial farmer-soldiers then marched down the hill to the North Bridge to the fife and drum strains of "The White Cockade." The Acton men, led by Captain Isaac Davis, were placed up front, in large part because they had muskets with bayonets, while Concord soldiers who followed did not.

The actual **Concord Fight** is described graphically by historian Robert Gross: As the Americans advanced, the three British companies brashly crowded the east end of the bridge. Some Redcoats tried briefly to pull up the planks. When the Americans grew near, the British fired a few warning shots, then a direct volley. "Their balls," said Amos Barrett, "whistled well." Isaac Davis and his company's young fifer, Abner Hosmer, fell dead. Major John Buttrick leaped into the air shouting, "Fire, fellow soldiers, for God's sake, fire!" The cry of "Fire! Fire!" flew through the ranks from front to rear. The resulting discharge wounded nearly a dozen of the enemy (including four British officers). Two Regulars were killed immediately, and another died later after being whacked on the skull with an axe by a young American farmer. (The British later claimed he – and others – had been scalped. However, these supposed atrocities had not actually taken place.)

The Provincials pressed on to cross the bridge; the British jammed together at the end, panicked and ran, unpursued to the town. The Concord Fight – "the shot heard round the world" – had actually taken a total of two to three minutes(Gross).

After crossing the bridge and regrouping behind a stone wall, the Americans had an opportunity to fire at Colonel Smith's troops as they returned from the Barrett Farm, but they held their fire. The British marched back to **Concord Center** and gathered in **Wright Tavern**, to eat, drink and to tend their wounded. After a total of four to five hours in Concord, at noon they began their retreat back to Boston.

The British retreat, also called the "Running Skirmish," began at **Meriam's Corner** in Concord. The British Regulars fought American snipers from 27 nearby towns. They faced the threat of total annihilation, which might have occurred had not they had been reinforced by over 1000 British Regulars of Lord Percy's relief troops, which marched from Boston and joined together with their exhausted comrades in Lexington to form a formidable force 1700 strong, who fought their way back to Charlestown and from thence back to Boston.

Concord Revolutionary Sites to Visit Today

★ **North Bridge today.** Visitors to the scene of the Concord Fight will arrive at the Minute Man National Historical Park, North Bridge Site, by foot, car or bus. They will walk down a tree shaded, stone wall lined path on the east bank towards the Concord River.

★ **The Concord Battle Monument**, a 25-foot granite obelisk erected in 1836, stands in front of the North Bridge. Its inscription commemorates "the first forcible resistance to British aggression." These words demonstrate that early Concordians were eager to differentiate the (alleged) historical distinction between the Concord Fight, where the Americans pursued the British and fired their muskets in anger and defiance, versus the Lexington Fight. At Lexington most of Captain Parker's militiamen were "dispersing" on the orders of the British. In later depositions by eye-witnesses, only two militiamen were confirmed to have returned British musket fire in defence (Ripley, French, Sawtell, Fischer).

It is ironic that this early Battle Monument was constructed at the site where the "invading army" – the British – stood.

★ **Graves of British Soldiers**. An engraved stone marker to the left of the Concord Battle Monument commemorates the two British soldiers who were killed (and buried) here, with an eulogy by poet James Russell Lowell: "They came three thousand miles and died/To keep the past upon its throne."

★ **Old North Bridge**. The current bridge is a graceful wooden replica of the original North Bridge that spans the Concord River. Its center is arched and its sturdy railings invite you to lean there at leisure, watch the slowly flowing water below and enjoy the pastoral views beyond. The original bridge was removed in 1793 and the site was empty until a Centennial bridge was constructed in 1875. The current bridge was built in 1956. While viewing the bucolic scene of the bridge and the tranquil river flowing below it, you can easily imagine yourself back in 1775.

★ **Concord Minuteman Statue**. As you cross over the bridge to the west bank of the Concord River you come up to the sculpture of the Minute Man, his left hand holding his plow and his right hand grasping his musket. The statue is the first major work sculpted by Concord's Daniel Chester French (1850-1931), who went on to create the imposing Lincoln Memorial statue in Washington, DC. The Minuteman statue was unveiled in 1875 at the Centennial celebration of the battle at the bridge at which 4,000 people cheered, including President Ulysses S. Grant and his cabinet. The inscription at the base is by Concord poet Ralph Waldo Emerson. Written in 1837, his "Concord Hymn" extolled the "shot heard round the world," which Emerson – much to the continued denials and consternation of another Middlesex town seven miles to the east – intended to specify had been fired from a musket at Concord's North Bridge.

★ A curving path up a gentle slope with a lovely vista of the river valley below leads to the **North Bridge Visitor Center** of the Minute Man National Historical Park. Within the original Stedman Buttrick House (1911) there is a diorama of the battle, items of historic interest, an audio-visual presentation and a book shop. Those who don't relish the hilly walk can drive there via Liberty Street from Monument Street.

★ After visiting the North Bridge, tourists should stop at the nearby **Old Manse** (meaning Minister's House in Scottish). This was constructed in 1770 by Rev. William Emerson, Ralph Waldo Emerson's grandfather. Rev. Emerson viewed the battle of the North Bridge from the windows of his house (Ripley). Since the house remained in the Emerson-Ripley family for almost 170 years, many of the furnishings are original, dating to the 1700s. The Old Manse is also famous as the house to which Nathaniel Hawthorne (1804-1864) took his bride Sophia Peabody Hawthorne of Salem to live from 1842-5. Here he wrote his second collection of short stories, "Mosses from an Old Manse" (1846).

COURTESY OF THE CONCORD FREE PUBLIC LIBRARY

John Meriam House, Concord (1650-1700) is one of Concord's oldest houses. Near this house the "running skirmish" began.

★ A logical next step would be a walk around **Concord Center** to capture its pre-Revolutionary and Revolutionary ambiance, which still exists, amazingly little changed over the past two hundred years. Concord, called Musquetaquid by its Natives, was settled in 1636 after a meeting, where an agreement (or "concord") was reached for purchase by the Puritans, who had fled persecution in England, and Algonquian Natives.

★ What is now Concord Center was originally built around the **Mill Pond**, which formed when the Mill Dam was built in the 1600's to block the **Mill Brook**. Water from the Mill Pond flowed over the **Mill Dam** to power a grist mill. The British soldiers tossed the musket balls they confiscated on April 19, 1775 into the water of the Mill Pond. Still angry, but ever frugal Concordians retrieved them from the water the next day. Main Street is still called The Milldam (or Mill Dam) by some traditional Concordians.

★ At the head of **Monument Square** is the **Colonial Inn**, whose east end was built as a house by James Minot before 1716. The very charming Inn still accommodates guests and serves meals. Its comfortable bar and restaurant is a rendezvous spot for people from all over the Boston area and for visitors from around the world.

Main Street in Concord is shown in this contemporary photo. It has changed very little from the 1830's when Concord's original Mill Dam was replaced by a road.

★ **Hill Burying Ground** (c. 1635) at Bedford Street and Lexington Road overlooks Monument Square. In use after Concord's earliest settlement, it was located next to the village's first Meeting House (church). Concord's Revolutionary leaders buried here include Colonel James Barrett and Major John Buttrick, "post" (scout) Reuben Brown and

The Wayside (1717) was the home of Concord's Revolutionary muster master, Sameul Whitney.

Dr. John Cuming. The marble head stones are still well preserved and visitors can easily locate the graves of prominent Concordians.

★ **Wright Tavern** (1747) still stands near Monument Square. The Minutemen mustered here early on the morning of April 19, 1775. British troops gathered here in the afternoon to tend their wounded, rest, and eat before they retreated to Charlestown and Boston. It now houses the Concord Chamber of Commerce.

★ A short walk down Lexington Road is the white-spired **First Parish Church** (1901). At this site, in a prior church building, the First Provincial Congress met in Concord in 1774 with John Hancock as President. The Congress in 1774 assigned Colonel James Barrett to supervise the collection and storage of supplies and weapons for an army of 15,000 men. It was to seize and destroy these supplies and weapons that British General Thomas Gage ordered his Regulars to (secretly) march to Concord in 1775. This Congress also authorized the formation of the Minutemen to train and be ready at a minute's notice.

★ **"The American Mile"** Historic District: This historic stretch along Lexington Road has some of America's oldest houses. It is comprised of a row of clapboard colonial houses built by Concord's first settlers in the 1600's and 1700's. At the time Lexington Road was called the Bay Road, since it led twenty miles eastward to Boston on Massachusetts Bay. Then Bay Road served as Concord's main street, as it did for almost 200 years. After the demolition of the Mill Dam in the 1820's what had been a causeway on top of the Mill Dam was rebuilt as Main Street. Originally houses on the Bay Road had shops on the ground floor and family living quarters on the second floor. Today these antique houses, are all privately owned and occupied:

★ **The Peter Bulkely/ Reuben Brown House** (c. 1667) at 77 Lexington Road belonged to Concord's first minister and later to the saddlemaker, Reuben Brown, who served as scout on April 19, 1775, carrying the first news of the Redcoats' arrival in Lexington to his anxious comrades in Concord. Brown worked in his saddlery on the ground floor and lived with his family on the second story.

★ **The Concord Museum**, 200 Lexington Road, displays artifacts and furnishings of Concord history from early Indian encampments to the first settlers in 1636 to Revolutionary times (including Paul Revere's lantern and Revolutionary muskets and powderhorns), and from Concord's literary lights of the mid 1800s, Emerson, Thoreau, Alcott, and Hawthorne. "Why Concord?" is a six gallery exhibition, film and interpretive program, which explains why so many important historic and literary events all occurred in the small village of Concord over many different eras.

★ **The Wayside** (c. 1717), 455 Lexington Road, is open to the public and is part of the Minute Man NHP. It was originally the home of Samuel Whitney, muster master of the Concord militia during the Revolution. Later it was the home of reformer Bronson Alcott and his daughter, Louisa May, and still later to authors Nathaniel Hawthorne and then writer Harriett Lothrop (pen name Margaret Sidney).

★ **Orchard House** (c. 1672) at 399 Lexington Road, was originally home to Concord's first lawyer, John Hoar. In 1676 he negotiated the ransom agreement for Mrs. Mary Rowlandson, the Lancaster minister's wife, who had been captured and held by the Indians for 15 months. Hoar's descendents were Revolutionary War soldiers, lawyers and statesmen. Orchard House is most famous as the home of Louisa May Alcott (1832-1888), the author of "Little Women," which is still popular today. She lived in this house

Orchard House is best known as the home of Louisa May Alcott and her family.

from 1858 to 1877 with her father, Bronson Alcott and with her mother and three sisters (her models for the sisters in "Little Women.") Orchard House is open to the public daily throughout the year.

★ At **Meriam's Corner** occurred the start of the "running skirmish," the British retreat from Concord to Boston. The **John Meriam House** (ca. 1650-1700) at 663 Lexington Road is one of the oldest houses in Concord.

★ **Colonel James Barrett's House** (1705) at 448 Barrett's Mill Road was built by Colonel Barrett, who was leader of Concord's militia. It was used to hide munitions and supplies, making it one of the objectives of the British march to Concord on April 19, 1775. Today it is privately owned and not open to the public.

★ In **Concord**, there is a colorful **Patriot's Day Parade**, featuring Minutemen companies from many nearby towns and Redcoat companies in historic dress. There is a battle reenactment at the North Bridge. On Patriot's Day (April 19th), there is a 6:00 a.m. dawn salute. The First Parish Church bell tolls, announcing the arrival of a horseman portraying Dr. Samuel Prescott, who has just ridden all the way from Boston to sound the alarm that the Regulars are fast approaching. There is also call to arms and a 21-gun salute near the North Bridge by the Concord Independent Battery (from their two horse-drawn cannons) and the Concord Minutemen.

Concord Minute Men

★ First activated on January 17, 1775, the current company of **Concord Minutemen** was reactivated in 1962 with the purpose of perpetuating the memory of the Concord soldiers of 1775 by participating in patriotic, civic, historic and educational events, as re-enactors and participants in "living history." In addition to ceremonial uniforms its members also wear Colonial period dress and carry appropriate replica weapons.

Sources:
Andrews, Joseph L., *Revolutionary Concord: The Shot Heard Round the World*, New Hampshire Sunday News, April 14, 1996; S.A.R. Magazine, Spring, 1997.
Concord Chamber of Commerce, *The Lexington-Concord Battle Road, Hour by Hour Account, April 19, 1775.*
Concord Historical Commission, *Highlights of Concord's Historic Resources*, 1995.
Fenn, Mary, *Old Houses of Concord*, D.A.R. 1974.
Fischer, David H., *Paul Revere's Ride*, Oxford, 1994.
French, Allen, *Historic Concord and the Lexington Fight*, Concord Free Public Library, 1992.
Galvin, John R. *The Minutemen- Their First Fight: Myths and Realities of the American Revolution*, Brassey, 1967 and 1989.
Gross, Robert, *The Minutemen and Their World*, Hill and Wang, 1976.
Sawtell, C. (Editor), *The Nineteenth of April, 1775, A Collection of First Hand Accounts*, N.P.S., 1991.
Massachusetts Soldiers, *Narrative of the Excursion and Ravages of the Kings' Troops and Their Depositions*, April. 1775 (Reprinted by New England and Virginia Company).
Revere, Paul, *Three Accounts of His Famous Ride*, Massachusetts Historical Society, 1976.
Ripley, Rev. Ezra, *A History of the Fight at Concord on the 19th of April, 1775, 1832.*
Russel, E.,(Editor), *Bloody Butchery by the British Troops or the Runaway Fight of the Regulars (The so called "Coffin Broadside")*, Salem Gazette, April 21, 1775.
Shattuck, Lemuel, *History of the Town of Concord*, 1832 (Reprinted by Higginson).

★ ★ ★ ★

Bedford's Contributions to the Cause

BY JOHN E. FILIOS AND JOSEPH L. ANDREWS, JR.

et up Nat Page! The Regulars are out!" The knocking on his door was persistent.

Nathaniel Page, a young Bedford Minuteman, was roused out of bed abruptly before dawn on April 19th, 1775. The alarm message was sent by Captain John Parker in Lexington and carried by Nathan Monroe and Benjamin Tidd on their fleet horses. They galloped to Bedford, where they stopped at Page's house first. As Page left his house he took the old Bedford flag with him. Then he headed for the Fitch Tavern, less than a half mile away (Brown, Fischer).

At the time Bedford was a small farming village of 482 people northwest of Boston, bordering Lexington to the south, Lincoln to the west and Concord to the north. The Bedford Minutemen gathered first at Fitch Tavern in Bedford's center for a hurried breakfast of cold cornmeal mush. Their leader, Captain Jonathan Wilson, was reported to say, "It's a cold breakfast, boys, but we'll give the British a hot dinner. We'll have every dog of them before night!" The men mustered under a spreading oak at the junction of Concord, Lexington and North roads, near today's Wilson Park.

One half mile down the Concord Road, the 50 man Bedford militia company, commanded by John Moore had already departed and were headed for Concord's Wright's Tavern six miles away. Many men in the militia were veterans, who had

The **Fitch Tavern** served as the meeting palce for Bedford's militia company on April 19, 1775.

fought with the British Army in the French and Indian War, which ended in 1763. Some in town doubted their loyalty to the rebel cause, if an actual armed conflict came to pass, since they were on King George's pay roll. But they were to prove their total support for the Patriot's cause later that day.

Bedford's 50 militia men were soon to joined by 27 Bedford Minutemen in Concord. Together Bedford's 77 farmer-soldiers formed about a fifth of the total American forces, the largest contingent of any town that gathered on Punkatasset Hill overlooking the North Bridge at dawn, awaiting the arrival of the British troops (Brown).

Abram Brown, the nineteenth century Bedford historian, relates a story that he heard from his friend, Cyrus Page, Nathaniel Page's grandson, as part of the Page family tradition: "On the arrival of the (Bedford) Company in Concord, they assisted in removing the stores (weapons, munitions and food at Col. Barret's farm) to places of greater safety. Tradition says that Cornet (flag bearer) Nathaniel Page laid down his flag and went to work, and when returning to look for it 'found the boys had got it and were playing soldiers.'" The Page family (oral) tradition also claims that Cornet Page carried the Bedford flag with him at the subsequent battle at the North Bridge (Brown). However, today many historians are skeptical of this claim, because of the absence of contemporary written descriptions about any American flag being observed at the battle scene.

The Bedford men followed the men of Acton and Concord down the hill at about 9:30 A.M. to clash with the British at the North Bridge, (as is described in detail in other chapters in this book about Concord and Acton.)

Bedford's contribution to the American pursuit of the British army along the Battle Road from Concord to Boston is described thusly by Abram Brown: "Bedford men were in pursuit of the retreating enemy. They left the Great Fields at Meriams Corner, and engaged in the attack, then hastened in the pursuit, and were in the thickest of the fight near Brook's Tavern (in Lincoln), where Captain Wilson was killed and Job Lane wounded..."(Brown). Job Lane of the militia, whose house can be visited today, was crippled by the musket ball that hit his hip.

Maxwell Thompson, a drover who was related to Captain Wilson by marriage, wrote later that he had joined the Concord Fight in April and did not return to his home in Bedford until after the Bunker Hill battle in June. Apparently, many of other Bedford citizen-soldiers did the same, joining the newly assembled Continential Army, which surrounded the British in the Siege of Boston.

The Bedford Flag

Perhaps no other historical artifact relating to the Revolution in the Boston area is more a source of intense local pride and also of extreme controversy than the "Bedford Flag." There is a flag today in Bedford claimed to be the one that may have been carried into battle by Nathaniel Page.

As described by Sharon McDonald of the staff of the Bedford Free Library and by Barbara Hitchcock in her recent book "The Bedford Flag," exactly when the flag was made, is like the shroud of Turin, cloaked in mystery. A sketch with a strikingly similar design, a mailed (armored) arm emerging from a cloud and grasping a sword, is to be found in seventeenth century herald-painter's sketch book preserved in London's British Library. The order is for a crimson silk cavalry flag for New England. The words on the flag sketch read, "Tre County Trom." A nearby note is dated 1665.

The Bedford Flag may have been carried by Bedford men in 1775 at the Concord Fight, although much controversy exists about its origins and its history. Here Leaders of Friends of the Bedford Flag, Jan van Steenwijk and Barbara Hitchcock, proudly display a replica of the flag with the help of a Bedford Minuteman.

If the Bedford flag is actually the flag in the London sketch book, then it could have been sent across the sea to Massachusetts to serve as the standard for the Three County Troop, which included militia men from Suffolk, Essex and Middlesex Counties. However, the fact that the Bedford flag's inscription reads "Vince Aut Morire" (Conquer or Die) and that modern silk experts feel that the damask pattern is more consistent with the early 1700's rather than the mid-1600's, render the origins of the Bedford flag uncertain (Hitchcock).

Was the flag actually carried by Cornet Nathaniel Page at the battle of the North Bridge, as his grandson Cyrus Page asserted, based on tales he heard as a boy that had been passed from father to son to grandson? Or are we to conclude, due to the absence of contemporary documentary descriptions, that the flag was not really present at the Concord Fight?

We do, however, have undisputed documentary evidence of why the flag that is now in the Bedford Library vault is missing its silver fringe. Nathaniel Page's youngest daughter, Ramunah, admitted that, " I took that silver fringe from that old flag when I was a giddy girl, and trimmed a dress for a military ball. I was never more sorry for anything than that which resulted in the loss of the fringe" (McDonald).

In later years the Bedford flag <u>did</u> fly at Concord on April 19, 1875, during the centennial celebration of the Concord Fight. Its last appearance in Concord was a dramatic one. On April 19, 1925 World War I doughboy veterans displayed the venerated Bedford flag from an open car driven through the streets of Concord.

Now the holy relic resides safely in a vault below the floors of the Bedford Free Library. There are plans to display the flag more openly in a new Library wing.

Job Lane House (c. 1713), one of Bedford's earliest homes, was occupied by the Lane family, including a Revolutionary War soldier, for over 130 years.

Bedford Minutemen

In 1964, a company of Bedford Minutemen was re-established by the Bedford Board of Selectmen to keep alive the spirit of 1775. They adopted a uniform similar to those worn by officers in Washington's Continental Army. They march at events to commemorate Bedford's rich Revolutionary heritage (Farrington).

Bedford's Historic Sites

★ **Job Lane House** (c. 1713) at 295 North Road is one of Bedford's earliest homes. Built as a salt box type house to house Lane's 11 children, it was enlarged by succeeding generations, whose additions were in different period styles, including Georgian and Federal. The home stayed in the Lane family for over 130 years. Since 1973, it has been owned by the Town of Bedford. In a creative approach to the challenge of affordably preserving a historic building, many Bedford organizations have each adopted a room, which they have helped to restore and maintain. These groups include the Bedford Minutemen, Historical Society, Garden Club, Rotary, and Boy and Girl Scouts. Friends of the Job Lane House conduct guided tours from May to October on alternate Sunday afternoons.

★ **Fitch Tavern** (c.1731) on Great Road near Town Hall is where the Bedford Minutemen rallied at dawn on April 19, 1775, before marching to the battle at Concord's North Bridge. The building is privately owned and not open to the public.

Sources:
Brown, Abram E., History of Bedford, 1891 and Beneath Old Rooftrees, 1896.
Brown, L.K., Wilderness Town, 1968.
Farrington, Williston, The Flag of the Minutemen, Bedford Minuteman Company, 1996.
Fischer, David H., Paul Revere's Ride, Oxford, 1994.
Hitchcock, Barbara, The Bedford Flag: A National Treasure, Friends of the Bedford Flag, 1998.
McDonald, Sharon, The Bedford Flag (brochure), Bedford Free Public Library, 1995.
Wharton, Virginia, The Bedford Sampler: Centennial Edition, 1974.

★ ★ ★ ★

Acton: "I Haven't A Man Who Is Afraid To Go!"

BY ELIZABETH S. CONANT, DAVID W. STONECLIFFE, AND JOSEPH L. ANDREWS

n the morning of April 19th 1775, believing that British troops were setting fire to the town of Concord, American officers ordered their militia and Minutemen to advance across the North Bridge towards the waiting muskets of the British. Colonel James Barrett instructed Major John Buttrick to find a company to take the lead in this dangerous endeavor. He asked a Concord captain, who declined. Buttrick then asked Acton's Captain Isaac Davis if he was afraid to go. Davis was heard to reply, "No, I am not and I haven't a man who is afraid to go!" The brave actions of Captain Davis and his men at this crucial juncture in American history led subsequent generations of Acton residents to characterize the events of the day as "the battle of Lexington, fought in Concord, by men of Acton."

Acton's defiance of the British Crown had slowly gathered momentum in the preceding years. In 1772 Acton men replied to Boston's Committee of Correspondence, noting alarming violations of the colonists' Royal charter of rights and privileges. They petitioned for the removal of British Governor Thomas Hutchinson, who personified their grievances. In 1773, after the Boston Tea Party protest, Acton and other Massachusetts towns passed resolutions condemning the actions of the Crown.

ACTON HISTORICAL SOCIETY

Minutemen Leaving the Home of Captain Issac Davis, April 19, 1775 in Acton, is the title of this scene painted by Acton artist Arthur Fuller Davis in 1894.

★ ACTON ★

On October 3, 1774 a special Acton Town Meeting chose delegates for the First Provincial Congress, held in defiance of the prohibitions of the British King and Parliament in London, which had passed the retaliatory "Intolerable Acts." Acton thus defied the Royal Governor in Boston, who was charged with enforcement These new coercive Acts banned public Town Meetings, which the American colonists felt were among their most treasured rights as Englishmen, guaranteed by Royal charter. Thus, October 3, 1774 marks a crucial turning point, the day Acton cast its lot with other American Patriots against the British King and the authority of his appointed representative, the Royal Governor in Boston. October 3 is still celebrated in Acton today as **Crown Resistance Day**.

In 1775 Acton was a farming village of approximately 750 people. Acton volunteers formed two companies of militia and one of Minutemen. In theory the militia companies, under the command of Colonel Francis Faulkner and Captain Joseph Robbins, were under orders from the Crown. In practice, as the years passed, this ceased to be true.

In November 1774, a company of Minutemen was organized in Acton through volunteer enlistment. Isaac Davis, a gunsmith by trade, was elected Captain. Davis's Minuteman company was particularly noted for its zeal. It met twice weekly for drill to the accompaniment of fifes and drums. A popular colonial tune, "The White Cockade" became the recognized musical signature of the company.

On the fateful morning of April 19th, Concord's Dr. Samuel Prescott, escaped after being captured by British soldiers in Lincoln on the road from Lexington. Galloping furiously, he spread the alarm to Concord at about 1 A.M., and then to Acton and Stow at about 2-3 A.M. Prescott's first stop in Acton was at the home of Captain Joseph Robbins. He did not dismount, but pounded against the clapboards and shouted, "Captain Robbins, Captain Robbins! The Regulars are coming!" He then raced on to alert Colonel Francis Faulkner in South Acton, and thence to neighboring Stow.

Captain Robbins rushed from the house with his musket and fired three shots as rapidly as he could reload. This was the signal for each Acton Minuteman and militiaman to report to the home of his captain, armed and prepared to march to Concord. The alarm was picked up and the sound of three musket shots could soon be heard repeated across the countryside. John Robbins, the Captain's thirteen year old son, mounted the family mare and rode off to carrying the news to Captain Davis and to Captain Simon Hunt, who led the Faulkner Company.

Thirty-seven Acton Minutemen arrived at Captain Davis's house before dawn on April 19, 1775, each outfitted with musket and bayonet, powder horn, bullet pouch, and a ration of bread and cheese. The march to Concord began to the familiar tune of "The White Cockade."

The last time the Minutemen companies had mustered in Concord, it had been on Concord's Common. But as Captain Davis and his men reached Barrett's Mill Road in Concord on the fateful day of April 19,1775, they were told that Colonel James Barrett, who was in general command of the militia at Concord, had

ACTON HISTORICAL SOCIETY

The Acton Center Issac Davis Minutemen's Monument dedication on October 29, 1851 was an elaborate ceremony, during which the bones of Acton martyrs Davis, Hosmer and Hayward, were moved from a cemetary to be re-buried at the base of this monument.

ordered his men to climb to the top of Punkatasset Hill above the west side of the Concord River overlooking the North Bridge. The Acton Minutemen joined him there. As on muster days, the companies took up their positions, militia on the left, Minutemen companies on the right facing the North Bridge.

In the meantime, the British expedition of about 700 Redcoats, marching from Boston and Lexington, had reached Concord. A British raiding force was ordered to cross the Concord River at the North Bridge and to proceed to Barrett's farm to seize weapons and burn supplies that they had been informed by spies were hidden in Colonel Barrett's barn. While the Colonials watched from their vantage point on Punkatasset Hill, seven companies of British Regulars reached the North Bridge. Four of these companies crossed the bridge and proceeded to Barretts's farm two miles distant, while the other three Regular companies remained to guard the bridge.

Soon after the arrival of Acton's company, led by Captain Davis, the Colonial officers called the first council of war in what was to become the American Revolution. Colonel Barrett was in command. Rumors of shooting and killing in Lexington earlier that morning were spreading, but the stories were confused and unverified. As the officers conferred, the assembled American militiamen saw smoke rising below in the distance over the town of Concord. Thinking the British were setting fire to Concord, the Colonial officers decided to cross the North Bridge to save the town.

★ ACTON ★

Colonel Barrett ordered Major John Buttrick to have his soldiers march forward down the hill and advance toward the bridge and into the town, but not to fire unless fired upon. It was then that Captain Davis agreed to have his men take the lead, because, as Davis asserted, "I haven't a man who is afraid to go!" (In later years a soldier who was at the scene claimed that the Acton men were placed in the front ranks because they were the only town company that was equipped with bayonets.) Davis's Acton company marched down toward the bridge, followed by three companies from Concord, the Acton company led by Simon Hunt, a Bedford company, a Lincoln company, and then the Robbins company from Acton.

As the Colonists approached, the British Redcoats guarding the west side of the North Bridge retreated over the bridge. They left behind a few Regulars, who began to tear up the planks from the bridge. Major Buttrick shouted at them to stop. The British fell back with their comrades to the east bank of the river to form a line for firing their muskets. When the American column was about 160 feet from the bridge, the Redcoats fired a few random warning shots. One ball creased the forehead of Luther Blanchard, the Acton fifer, slightly wounding him and a Concord militiaman in the ranks behind. Major Buttrick then gave the order to the Americans to return fire: "Fire fellow soldiers; for God's sake fire!"

The Acton men, who led the American farmer-soldiers were in the front ranks and thus, were the only Colonials who were in a position to fire. As they lifted their muskets, a volley was fired by the British. Acton's Isaac Davis was killed instantly. Abner Hosmer, also of Acton, was mortally wounded with a bullet through his head. Thus, ironically the Acton farmer-soldiers, who had volunteered to lead the Americans by marching down the hill in their front ranks towards the bridge, in what was later dubbed "the first forcible resistance to the might of the British Empire," also gained the distinction of becoming the **only** Americans killed at the skirmish at North Bridge, later known as the "Concord Fight."

The volley returned by the Minutemen killed one Redcoat, fatally wounded two others, and wounded several more, including four British officers. The British retreated toward Concord, followed by a few colonists. But the colonists were disorganized. About 200 gathered on Ripley Hill to watch the British, but most of the others returned to the bridge. The bodies of Davis and Hosmer were carried up the hill to Major Buttrick's home, and were taken back to the Davis home in Acton later that day.

Isaac Davis' widow Hannah, who was left with four children, the youngest about fifteeen months of age, described that fateful day in a deposition sixty years later: "The alarm was given early in the morning, and my husband lost no time in making ready to go to Concord.

"My husband said but little that morning. He seemed serious and thoughtful; but never seemed to hesitate as to the course of his duty. As he led the company from the house, he turned himself round and seemed to have something to communicate. He said only 'take good care of the children,' and was soon out of sight.

"In the afternoon he was brought home a corpse. He was placed in my bedroom till the funeral. His countenance was pleasant and seemed little altered.

"The bodies of Abner Hosmer, one of the company, and of James Hayward, one of the militia company, who was killed in Lexington (later that afternoon) were brought by their friends to the house, where the funeral of the three was attended together" (Deposition of the Wife of Capt. Davis before Justice of the Peace Francis Tuttle, August 14, 1835).

As the war progressed more Acton men enlisted. Twenty-three were at Bunker Hill on June 17, 1775. Josiah Hayward was sent to represent the town in the Provincial Congress, which began to prepare for a long campaign. By December, quotas of military supplies were assigned to various towns. Acton was required to supply a ton of hay, ten blankets, and thirteen more men.

In the spring of 1776 the idea of independence from England spread through the colonies. The redress of grievances and guarantee of civil rights were no longer enough. Acton voters went on record in their town meeting of June 14, 1776 as believing that "the present age will be Defiant in their duty to God, their posterity, and themselves if they Do not Establish an American Republic..."

Acton Remembers Today

Acton residents continue to honor their rich heritage. The Acton Minutemen of today march in commemoration of Captain Isaac Davis and his company of thirty-eight men The group was reactivated as the Acton Militia in 1963 and takes part in many town and area celebrations.

Each year on the 19th of April the Acton Minutemen again march along the original trail from the Davis homestead to the Concord bridge, a distance of about eight miles. In recent years they have been followed by thousands of participants, including American serviceman, area students and Boy and Girl Scouts, who have participated in the march. Upon completing their trek on the **"Isaac Davis Trail,"** each marcher is awarded a scroll, a historic map of the route, commemorating the event.

Acton Minutemen marching in a Patriots' Day parade.

The Acton Minutemen then participate along with uniformed Minutemen and militia units from many Massachusetts towns, who march through the streets of Concord to the North Bridge in Concord's annual Patriots' Day Parade.

Revolutionary Era Sites to Visit Today in Acton

★ **The Hosmer House (1760)**, 300 Main Street, is a restored saltbox farmhouse. It was built for Jonathan Hosmer, a bricklayer, whose younger brother Abner was killed at the North Bridge fight in 1775, and his bride Submit Hunt. It was later enlarged for their son Simon and his wife Sarah in 1797. It is owned and operated by the Acton Historical Society and open to the public for teas and tours on a limited basis.

★ The **Jenks Library**, also at 300 Main Street, behind the Hosmer House, contains the Acton Historical Society's archives of historic Acton papers, maps and pictures and is open to the public by appointment.

★ The **Faulkner Homestead (1707)** at 5 High Street is the oldest house still standing in Acton. It was the house of Colonel Francis Faulkner, who commanded one of Acton's three militia companies. In the front yard of the house, Acton's Provincial militia mustered and then marched off to the Concord Fight on April 19, 1775. It was the homestead for six generations of the Faulkner family for 202 years (1728-1940). Today it is owned by the Iron Work Farm of Acton, a historic preservation organization, and is open the fourth Sunday of the month or by appointment.

★ The **Isaac Davis Monument (1851)** on Main Street in Acton Center on the green opposite Town Hall is a tall stone obelisk. At the its base are buried the three Acton men killed on April 19, 1775, Captain Isaac Davis and Abner Hosmer (slain at Concord's North Bridge) and James Hayward (later killed in Lexington). Their bodies were moved here from burying grounds elsewhere in Acton at an elaborate dedication ceremony in 1851.

Sources:
Acton Historical Society (Elizabeth S. Conant and David W. Stonecliffe, Editors),
A Brief History of Acton, 1974.
Hamlin, Rev. Cyrus, My Grandfather Colonel Francis Faulkner and My Uncle Francis
Faulkner, Jr. in the Battle of Lexington, Boston, 1887. (Reprinted in 1983.)
Fischer, David H., Paul Revere's Ride, Oxford, 1994.

★ ★ ★ ★

Sudbury's April Morning

BY JAY CANNON

 udbury, a quiet farming community west of Boston, was incorporated as a town in 1639. It was named after the town of Sudbury in Suffolk, England.

After events such as the terrible massacre in Boston during the cold winter night of March 5, 1770 and the raid on the powder house in Somerville in September of 1774, Sudbury citizens felt they needed to be ready to act. They felt the tensions building up with the British. Accordingly, in November of 1774, the citizens of Sudbury voted to recommend to the militia companies to elect officers and hold them in readiness for protection of their town and country against any aggression from the Crown. It didn't take long for men of Sudbury to elect officers. Those companies and officers are shown in the table at the end of the chapter.

All companies were under the command of Lieutenant Colonel Ezekiel How. By March of 1775, most men were equipped with useable firelocks, flints, bayonets, one pound of powder, cartridge boxes and about two pounds of lead, enough to make about 30 or so musket balls. Those not as well equipped carried pitchforks, hatchets, and even clubs. They knew how to use their flintlocks as well as any

COURTESY OF WAYSIDE INN, SUDBURY

The Wayside Inn in Sudbury.

TWENTY FOUR SHILLINGS

Issued in defence of American Liberty

Ense petit placidam, sub Libertate Quietem

MAGNA CHARTA

Aug^t: 18.1775.

Redcoat. During the cold winter months they drilled in the barns with mittens on. As the time came closer to a confrontation with the King's troops, they drilled weekly and honed their shooting skills. They were ready.

Then it happened! During the early morning of April 19, 1775, between 3 o'clock and 4 o'clock in the morning, Dr. Abel Prescott, Jr., an alarm rider sent from Concord by his brother, Dr. Samuel Prescott, awoke Thomas Plimpton, who lived in Sudbury Center. Plympton was a member of the Committee of Correspondence and the Provincial Congress. Plympton awoke the church sexton around 4:30 a.m. He instructed him to ring the alarm bell and discharge his musket. Another messenger woke Captain Nixon's household shouting, "Up, up! The Redcoats are up as far as Concord!"

By sunrise, Sudbury Center was a frenzy of activity. Alarm riders dashed off to warn the other towns. Drummers beat out assembly as men fell into ranks. Wives and mothers helped husbands and sons with last minute preparations. Dogs barked as horses stomped and snorted. Young men not quite sure of what could happen wondered what the day would bring. Others, being veterans of the French and Indian War, knew full well that some of their neighbors might die shortly. Soon they were off... Lieutenant Colonel How and Captains Nixon and Haynes leading the north militia and minute companies towards Concord with the sounds of fifes and drums lifting spirits in the warm April morning. The East Side Sudbury Companies also repeated this scene. They headed off towards Concord by way of Lincoln.

As Captains Nixon and Haynes' companies were within one half mile of the Concord South Bridge, they were intercepted by Stephen Barrett. Barrett was the son of Colonel James Barrett, commander of the Concord Militia Companies. Stephen said companies of Redcoats were already holding the South Bridge. The minute and militia companies were ordered to detour around the South Bridge and head towards Concord's North Bridge. As Lieutenant Colonel How spoke with his captains about the situation, eighty year old Deacon Josiah Haynes grew restless and said to Captain Nixon, "If you don't go and drive them British from the bridge, I shall call you a coward."

Trying to quell Haynes' impatience, Nixon replied, "I should rather be called a

British Redcoat re-enactors march over Concord's North Bridge. On April 19, 1775. The Redcoats retreated from Concord. Sudbury militia and Minutemen were among the Colonial forces that were involved in fierce fighting along the Battle Road that day.

coward by you than called to account by my superiors for disobedience of orders." Cooler heads prevailed and the companies detoured around South Bridge, avoiding an immediate conflict.

While on the way to the North Bridge, the column approached the farm house of Colonel James Barrett. The Sudbury men spied three companies of British soldiers at Barrett's house. Soldiers under the command of Captain Parsons were ordered to ransack Barrett's home for hidden military stores. Finding some wooden gun carriages, the Redcoats dragged the good carriages to the front yard and set them ablaze. Upon seeing the blaze, Lieutenant Colonel How roared "If any blood has been shed, not one of the rascals shall escape!"

Wanting a closer look, How removed his sword and ventured up to Barrett's house as if he was just passing by. Stopped by the British soldiers, he was asked where he was going. "Down along on some business and should not like to be detained," How stated matter-of-factly. The British soldiers, not suspecting him of any wrong doing, let him pass unharmed. How, seeing that no harm had come to the Barrett family, proceeded along his way. The Sudbury companies, seeing this, detoured around the Redcoats and joined the stream of minute and militia units from other towns mustering just above the North Bridge.

★ SUDBURY ★

After the British started removing planks from the North Bridge and smoke was seen rising from the town, over 450 Provincials were on the move, over the North Bridge to Concord Center, in hopes of protecting the town from certain destruction by Crown Forces. They met the British soldiers at the North Bridge and shots were exchanged.

The British then retreated from the North Bridge and regrouped in Concord Center. After about a two and a half hour rest in the center, they started their fateful march back to Boston. About half past twelve in the afternoon, at Meriam's Corner, as the British crossed a small bridge, shots were fired by a few minutemen at the rear of the British column. The British rear guard turned and fired. With this British volley, Provincial muskets started sniping at the British column from all sides. Soldiers from East Sudbury, commanded by Captain Joseph Smith, situated on the south side of Meriam's corner, joined in the firing. Two British soldiers were killed and several officers wounded, including Ensign Jeremy Lester.

About a mile and a half from Merriam's Corner the British passed Brooks Tavern. British officer, Lt. Sutherland stated, " Here I saw upon a height upon my right hand a vast number of armed men drawn out in Battalia order (battle line), I dare say near 1000 who on our coming nearer dispersed into the woods." Nearly 500 Provincials from Framingham and the Sudbury Company of Captain Nathaniel Cudworth became engaged with the British here at Hardy's (Brooks) Hill. As the British charged up the hill towards the men hidden in the woods, deadly provincial musketry drove the British back. Sudbury Minute and militiamen fought on both sides of the road at Hardy's Hill. One young man recalled, "I was running across a lot where there was a bend in [the] road in order to get a fair shot, at the enemy, in company with a Scotsman who was in Braddock's defeat 19 year before, after we had discharged our guns I observed the Scot who appeared very composed I wished I felt as calm as he appeared to be." The old Scot, named John Weighton, replied to the young lad, "It's a Tread to be Larnt." Weighton had been in seven battles and this was his eighth.

As the sun set on April 19th, 1775, people reflected, buried their dead and bandaged their wounded. Sudbury lost two men. Feisty eighty year old Deacon Josiah Haynes, who dared call his superior a coward at the South Bridge in Concord, was killed by a British musket ball in Lexington nearly ten hours after the alarm rang in Sudbury Center. The second was Asahel Reed. He was a member of Captain Nixon's Minute Company. Both men are buried in the Old Burying Ground in Sudbury Center. Joshua Haynes who also was a member of Nixon's Minute Company was wounded. Lieutenant Elisha Wheeler had a horse shot out from under him and Thomas Plympton, also on horse, had a musket ball go through the fold of his coat without injury.

The men of Sudbury continued their service for their country during the American War for Independence. At Bunker Hill three Sudbury companies fought under the command of Colonel John Nixon, Major Nathaniel Cudworth and Adj. Abel Holden, Jr. When the British left Boston for good on March 17, 1776, the war had moved from the New England region into New York and points south. Many of the Sudbury men, as others from the many New England towns, stayed behind to tend their farms and care for their families. John Nixon was promoted to Brigadier General. Captains' Abel Holden, Caleb Clapp and Aaron Haynes continued their service. During the American Revolution, nearly five hundred men from a town of twenty one hundred served. Sudbury produced one brigadier general, three colonels, two majors, two adjutants, two surgeons, twenty-four captains and twenty-nine lieutenants. Twenty-six Sudbury men gave their lives for the American cause. Eight were wounded, including General John Nixon (then Colonel) at Bunker Hill. Four men, during the course of the war, were taken prisoner and were never heard from again.

Sudbury's Revolutionary Era Sites

★ **The Wayside Inn (1716)**, one of America's oldest operating inns, is located on the Old Boston Post Road (Route 20) in Sudbury. Poet Henry Wadsworth Longfellow made the inn famous in his "Tales of the Wayside Inn" (1863). More recently Henry Ford purchased the Wayside Inn and 1500 acres of land in 1923 and refurbished the inn. Ford also moved the Red Stone school house to the site from nearby Sterling. (Myth has it that the ditty "Mary Had a Little Lamb" was based on the tale of one Mary Sawyer bringing her lamb to this very school house. However, the Inn's historians today are dubious about this tale and say there is no solid evidence that Mary Sawyer was the Mary of the song.) Today the Inn provides

lodging, a restaurant, colonial tavern and gift shop. A chapel, popular for weddings, and a grist mill also stand on the Inn's spacious grounds.

★ **Sudbury Center Burying Ground** contains the statue of a Revolutionary War soldier. Standing among the weathered slate head stones is one that reads, "In memory of Deacon Josiah Haynes, who died in Freedom's Cause the 19th day of April, 1775 in the 79th year of his Age."

SUDBURY'S MILITIA COMPANIES AND OFFICERS
★ North Militia Company, West Side, Captain Aaron Haynes–60 men
★ East Militia Company, East Side, Captain Joseph Smith–75 men
★ South Militia Company, both Sides, Captain Moses Stone– 92 men
★ Troop of Horse, both Sides, Captain Isaac Loker–21 men
★ Minute Company, West Side, Captain John Nixon– 58 men
★ Minute Company, East Side, Captain Nathaniel Cudworth–40 men
★ Alarm Company, Captain Jabez Puffer (the men and boys who were
    too old or young to serve in the other companies)

Sources:
Fischer, David H., Paul Revere's Ride, Oxford, 1994.
French, The Day of Lexington and Concord, 1925.
Hudson, Alfred, The History of Sudbury, Massachussetts.
Powers, John C. , We Shall Not Tamely Give it Up, 1988.
Whitehill, Walter Muir, In Freedom's Cause, Lakeside Press.

★ ★ ★ ★

The Daughters
of Liberty

BY D. MICHAEL RYAN

 n the telling of our colonial history, often there is little mention of women and their roles in defining moments. Yet even surrounding the 19th April 1775 events, the daughters of America's liberty were visible and actively involved.

For example, might it be that the actions of two ladies were a major factor in the fight at Concord's North Bridge? **Margaret Kemble Gage**, American born wife of Boston's British military Governor Thomas Gage, was suspected of spying by both sides and harbored hopes that her husband's actions would not be the cause of blood-spilling. It is believed that she may have been the "spy" who leaked word of the Regulars' mission to Concord (Fischer).

At age 71, Concordian **Martha Moulton** was at home when the soldiers entered town. When sparks from burning captured materials caught the Town House roof on fire, Martha begged and harangued the British into extinguishing the blaze. Resulting smoke, observed by the Americans mustered near Buttrick's farm, caused them to march to the town's rescue precipitating the "shot heard 'round the world," and helping to ignite the American Revolution.

COURTESY OF THE MENOTOMY MINUTE MEN

Mother Bathericke accepts the surrender of British soldiers at a reenactment in Arlington (Menotomy).

★ WOMEN IN THE REVOLUTION ★

Various acts of bravery were inacted that day by women. **Mrs. Amos Wood**, Concord, saved military stores from British capture by insisting a locked room harbored women and, thus, it was left unopened.

Hannah Barron (also Barns, Burns), protected the Provincial Treasurer's chest filled with money and important papers by blocking soldiers' entrance to a tavern room, claiming it and the trunk to be hers.

Abigail Wright, wife of the Concord Tavern proprietor, is said to have secreted the Church communion silver in soap barrels to avoid their being stolen. The same tale is attributed to Mrs. Jeremiah Robinson, who supposedly gathered the silver, hid it in her basement soap barrels and barricaded her door against British intrusion.

Rebecca Barrett, wife of Concord's militia Colonel, helped hide military stores and equipment about the farm, then remained at home to protect family and property from the expected British invasion. She fed the searching soldiers upon request, but refused money thrown at her, commenting that "we are commanded to feed our enemy" and that their coins were "the price of blood". Rebecca's actions saved valuable military materials from discovery as well as her property from damage and her son from arrest.

Another Barrett woman, Rebecca's granddaughter **Meliscent**, age 15, had learned from a British officer how to roll powder cartridges. On the night of 18 April, she supervised young women of Concord in preparing these items, which were most likely used against the Regulars at North Bridge.

For most wives and mothers, it was a time of fear, trauma, uncertainty, terror and often sadness as their husbands and sons went off to fight. Yet the women contributed to freedom's stand as best they could. **Lydia Mulliken** of Lexington, watched her fiance, Dr. Samuel Prescott, ride off with Revere and Dawes to warn Concord of the British threat. During the enemy's retreat, the soldiers burned her house and shop.

Lincoln's **Mary Flint Hartwell**, hearing Dr. Prescott's night alarm for her Minuteman husband, handed their baby to a servant and ran a distance in the dark to warn Lincoln's Captain Smith of the approaching danger (for further information about her brave actions, see the chapter on Lincoln).

From her house near Lexington Green, **Ruth Harrington** watched her husband Jonathan (standing with Parker's company), struck by a British musket ball, crawl to their house and die at her feet.

From the Manse, in Concord, **Phoebe Bliss Emerson**, the Concord minister's wife, would watch in dismay the North Bridge fight and wonder after the welfare of her husband William.

Hannah Davis of Acton, like many wives, would see husband Isaac march to Concord, intuition telling her that she would never see him again. He died in the British volley at the Bridge.

In Menotomy (Arlington), **Mother Batherick** while digging dandelions accepted the surrender of six fleeing British soldiers with the admonishment "...tell King

George that an old women took six of his grenadiers prisoner."

Throughout the day, many women would gather family valuables and children then flee to neighboring towns or into nearby woods for protection from the marauding British.

Others like **Alice Stearns Abbott** remained at home (Watertown) and with her mother and sisters making cartridges and sending food for the army. Later she would write, "I suppose it was a dreadful day in our house and sad indeed for our brother, so dearly loved, never came home."

In Menotomy, **Mrs. Butterfield** would return home to find a bleeding, dying British officer in her bed. Though she was accused of being a Tory, she cared for him some 10 days until he died. When a neighbor threatened to kill the officer, Mrs. Butterfield protected him shouting, "Only cowards would want to kill a dying man."

Some women went to extraordinary lengths in liberty's cause. At Pepperell, following the men's departure for Concord, the women met, formed a military company, dressed as men, armed themselves and patrolled the town. **Prudence Cummings**, elected Captain, captured a Tory officer at gun point. Such exploits would set the stage for later female military heroes such as **Margaret Corbin** ("Captain Molly", 1776, Battle of Ft. Washington, NY, wounded/ captured); **Mary Ludwig Hays** ("Molly Pitcher", 1778, Battle of Monmouth, NJ); **Deborah Sampson** (Continental Army soldier 1782-83, disguised as a man, wounded twice).

Thus, from its earliest days, America's struggle for liberty and freedom was waged by and had great impact upon America's women, as well as its men. Such should never be overlooked, ignored or taken lightly.

Sources:
"Paul Revere's Ride" by David H. Fischer 1994.
"The Day of Concord and Lexington" by Allen French 1925.
"Concord: American Town" by Townsend Scudder 1947.
"History of Concord, Massachusetts." by Lemuel Shattuck 1835.
"We Were There!" by Vincent J-R Kehoe, 1974.
"Heroine of the Battle Road, Mary Hartwell" by Palmer Faran, Cottage Press, Lincoln, MA, 1995.

★ ★ ★ ★

Black Flutist is thought to be Revolutionary War soldier and fifer, Barzillai Lew (1743-1822) of Boston. This portrait, which hangs at the State Department in Washington, D.C. was formerly attributed to Gilbert Stuart.

★ ★ ★ ★

Black Americans' Battle for Freedom

BY D. MICHAEL RYAN

he Provincial Congress in Concord, April 1774, reflected upon "the propriety, that while we are attempting to free ourselves from our present embarrassments and preserve ourselves from slavery, that we also take into consideration the state and circumstances of the negro slaves."

On the eve of a revolution, which was fought in order to avoid "the horrors of British slavery" and "maintain the natural rights of men," some twelve Concord families owned slaves. This peculiar institution, part of town life since 1708, included at its height some 20 men, women and children. Better treated than their counterparts in some colonies, Concord slaves could exercise certain rights, had to be educated in the ways of God and religion, often were inclusive parts of the family they served and could obtain freeman status.

Historically, laws prohibited blacks from serving in militias, but they were often ignored during most 18th Century American colonial wars due to manpower shortages. With the master's consent, a slave could enter the military, but was rarely allowed to because of his great value to his owner.

A common fear among whites was that armed slaves might revolt. In 1768 this feeling was reinforced when a British officer was arrested in Boston for inciting blacks "to fight against their masters." In 1774, some Boston slaves supposedly offered their military service to British General Thomas Gage in exchange for their freedom. And even as their Minutemen and militia companies marched to the 19th April alarm, remaining Framingham citizens armed themselves in fear of a black uprising.

The first of the five protesting Americans killed by British musket fire at the Boston Massacre on March 5, 1773 was **Crispus Attucks**, who was of mixed African and Native American ancestry.

During the fall and winter of 1774, blacks (including Concordians) most likely did not drill with town militias. But, as spring approached, bringing with it the threat of armed conflict with England, volunteers were sought, which in some instances included blacks. While no official records list blacks as serving in Concord's companies by 1775, one roll call seems to indicate **Philip Barrett** (slave of Colonel James Barrett) present at a militia muster. Since he was only age fourteen, it is more likely that he only accompanied the Colonel but did not directly serve. This may also have been the case with several other Concord slaves.

In addition to Barrett, other town slave owners in 1775 included Tory and for-

Boston Massacre (1770), Crispus Attucks, of mixed African-American descent, was the first colonist killed by British musket fire.

mer slave trader Duncan Ingraham (**Cato**), Town Meeting moderator Dr./Col. John Cuming (**Brister**), and militia Capt. George Minot (**Caesar**). Other Concord slave masters included muster master Samuel Whitney (**Casey**), Ralph Waldo Emerson's grandfather and Concord's minister–the Reverend William Emerson (**Frank**). Deacon Simon Hunt (Caesar) and Tory religious activist– Dr. Joseph Lee (**Cato**). While these slaves may not have fought at North Bridge, some later did serve in the war.

A few records document the role of blacks fighting British Regulars alongside their white townsmen on April 19, 1775. **Prince Estabrook**, a member of Parker's Lexington militia, fought and was wounded at the Lexington Green. At Concord's North Bridge, **Caesar Jones** (with Lt. Timothy Jones), **Cambridge Moore** and **Caesar Prescott** fought in the Bedford ranks, and **Caesar Bason** (later killed at Breed's Hill) may have represented Westford. Numerous towns counted black men in their ranks as they marched to pursue the fleeing British troops eastward along the "Battle Road."

One Concord story of April 19th centers on **Cato Ingraham**, who stood at his owner's house, hands behind his back, as the Regulars approached. A British soldier (possibly Major Pitcairn?), believing Cato had a weapon, pointed a pistol to his head and demanded his arms. Unflustered, Cato raised his left, then his right arm, noting that those were the only arms he possessed.

Heroic tales of local people of color are recorded on April 19th, including stories of Menotomy's **Cuff Cartwright**, who ignored British bribes and rode to spread the alarm through town, and mulatto David Lamson, who led the old men of Metonomy in the capture of a British supply wagon.

Although maybe not involved at the North Bridge fight, Concord's blacks distinguished themselves in later military service. **Philip Barrett** marched in July 1775, enlisted in Captain Heald's company in 1779, served a six-month tour at West

Point and never returned to Concord. **Brister (Cuming) Freeman** served under Colonel John Buttrick at Saratoga in 1777, witnessed British General Burgoyne's surrender, enlisted again in 1779, and earned his freedom. He later returned to Concord, settled and married there. His burial site in Lincoln, next to five British soldiers, was noted by Thoreau in "Walden." **Caesar Minot** served in the Patriot army for three months in 1775 and then signed for a 3-year enlistment, returning to Concord at war's end. **Casey Whitney** fled snowballs and the threats of his owner's son, enlisted in the army, was later freed and also returned to live in Concord.

While many Concordians had opposed slavery and supported its abolition, a General Court resolve on the matter was vetoed in 1771 by Governor Hutchinson. By 1780, the Massachusetts State Constitution was ratified, but only after a Bill of Rights was added which included a ban on slavery.

The military role of Concord's slaves and freemen in the American Revolution should neither be ignored nor diminished. They fought to gain liberty for their nation, a struggle which helped them to gain their own freedom from slavery.

John Jack, perhaps Concord's most famous slave, because of the memorable epitaph on his tomb stone, is buried at the summit of the Old Hill Burying Ground near Monument Square in Concord Center. His epitaph, written in 1773 by Daniel Bliss, a Concord Tory, reads in part: "God wishes man free, man wills us slaves. I will as God wills; God's will be done."

Concord Blacks' Names and Places

Today we still see signs of black Concordians in the town's place names. **Jennie Dugan Road, Jennie Dugan Spring, Brister's Hill Road**, and **Peter Spring Road** are all named for the slaves who, after gaining their freedom, came to settle down in these parts of Concord.

Sources:
Piersen, William D., Black Yankees, 1988.
McManus, Edgar J., Black Bondage in the North, 1973.
Elliott, Barbara K and Jones, Janet W., Concord: Its Black History 1636-1860, Concord School Department, 1976.
Trumbull, Joan, Concord and the Negro, 1944.
Sabin, Douglas, The Role of Blacks in the Battle of April 19, 1775, Minute Man, National Historical Park, National Park Service, 1987 (Archives).

★ ★ ★ ★

"On the March:" Stockbridge Indian Marches to Boston. As early as April 11, 1775, Native American Mohegans from Stockbridge in Western Massachusetts, were considering communicating with the Provincial Congress, then meeting in Concord, to offer their services as fighters, to help relieve the British Siege of Boston. Their Chief, Solomon Uhhaunauwaunmut, wrote, "It appears blood must be spilled So, you will let me fight in my own Indian way" (Letter in the Massachusetts State Archives). On April 21, seventeen Mohegan braves left Stockbridge to walk to Boston to help the Patriots surrounding the British-held city. This sketch shows a Stockbridge Indian walking on the road to Boston. British Governor and General, Thomas Gage, wrote that during the siege, "their Indians and riflemen have been firing above six weeks" (Gage letter to William Tryon on September 10, 1775). Text and original sketch by Kenneth Hamilton, Native American artist and living history interpreter, 1999.

★ ★ ★ ★

Native Americans and the Revolutionary War

BY SHIRLEY BLANCKE

hat did American Indians in Eastern Massachusetts do in the American Revolution?

It has been suggested that the Revolutionary War cannot be understood properly without understanding American Indian participation. It was an anti-colonial war of liberation for Indian peoples too, but the threat to Native Americans' freedom often came from their colonial neighbors rather than from London, and American Indians' colonial experience did not end with American independence (Calloway).

The first Concord Native American whose name we know is Sagamore (chief) Tahattawan. He was one of Christian Minister John Eliot's earliest converts in the 1640's. His son, John was later a leader of the Christian Indian village of Nashoba (located in what is now Littleton). This is where Concord's Native people moved shortly after Concord was founded in 1635, after the new town's founders, settlers from England led by Simon Willard from Kent, declined the former inhabitants' request to live near by.

John Tahattawam married Sarah, daughter of another John, the Sagamore of Pawtucket, which means place of falls or rapids (present day Lowell). This place was located within the area of the Pawtucket tribe, that extended over the northern half of Massachussetts Bay. Sagamore John was probably a tribal sub-chief. The marriage provides us with the only hint we have of the Concord Indians' tribal identity (Pawtucket). But they could equally well have been Nipmuc or Massachusett. Concord itself was previously called Musketaquid, the place of the grassy or reedy river, referring to the extensive meadows and swamps bordering the Concord River, which today are part of Great Meadows National Wild Life Refuge.

Tahattawan and his community were descended from at least five thousand years of Algonquian-speaking forbearers, and before that from Native people who moved into the area at the end of the Ice Age, 10-12,000 years ago. These pioneers were hunters of mastodon and reindeer and traveled through a tundra environment. As the climate warmed, spruce woodland and mixed-oak forests appeared, supporting red deer and animal species, which are still here today. From about 7000 years ago onwards, waves of Indian settlers migrated along the rivers between the sea coast and inland forests, eventually establishing a pattern of seasonal movement. They stopped for a few months at a time in places where they could gather seasonally available foods. They hunted deer and raccoons, trapped beaver, as well as doing fishing and fresh water claming in the inland rivers and streams. They also gathered edible plants in the spring and summer and nuts in the fall.

Using modern techniques of radioactive carbon dating of charcoal remnants of ancient Native camp fires, archeologists today have determined that some later Native settlers lived in Concord approximately 4000 and 2500 years ago.

Not until about a thousand years ago did the Algonquians add farming to their long established customs of migratory hunting, fishing and gathering. They now stayed in one place long enough in the summer season to grow corn, squash, and beans. Later villagers would stay put for several years at time. Today visitors to the Great Meadows Wildlife Refuge in Concord can view hills on the south side and across the Concord River, which were once the locations of prehistoric Indian villages.

Two of the original nations/tribes that exist today are the Wampanoag, who still live in southeastern Massachusetts and Cape Cod, and the Nipmuc in central Massachusetts. Their language was Algonquian, which belonged to Native Americans of the eastern seaboard and mid-west. Their participation in the Revolutionary War has not been fully studied, but the information available suggests some parallelism of experience between Nipmuc and Wampanoag. Today's Mashpee Wampanoag, in particular are still experiencing the tragic effects of colonialism into this century.

A Revolutionary War recruitment list from Plymouth, on the Massachusetts coast south of Boston, identifies as Indian certain enlistees from Plymouth county, a Wampanoag area (Gardner). Eighteen men from 16 to 34 years of age were enlisted in five regiments: Lt. Col. White's, T. Cushing's, Major Cary's, Col. C.O. Cotton's, and Lt. Col. Hall's. Some of their names are unmistakably Native: Joshua Compsett, Parm Mouth, Benjamin Unket, Isaac Wickums, Samuel Word, and a 16 year-old drummer, Caesar Meria; and they came from eight towns: Bridgewater, Kingston, Marshfield, Middleborough, Pembroke, Plymouth, Rochester, and Scituate.

The Wampanoag community of Mashpee on Cape Cod suffered particularly heavily in the Revolutionary War. One Barnstable regiment lost 25 out of 26 men, and the total loss for Mashpee was half the male population (more than 50). By 1788 there were only 25 men and 110 women of unmixed aboriginal descent remaining in Mashpee. Before and during the war a different kind of struggle had also been taking place for control over Mashpee's land. In 1760, Reuben Cognehew, a Mashpee leader, traveled to England to complain to the newly enthroned George III that white guardians placed over them by the Massachusetts Legislature were forcing them to cede their land to white settlers, reducing the Mashpees to destitution. King George lll prevailed on the Legislature to give the Mashpees greater autonomy. But their short-lived freedom was lost after the Revolution, when the Mashpees became the equivalent of colonials for the newly liberated and independent dominant white Americans of

ARLINGTON HISTORICAL SOCIETY

The Hunter, Menotomy Indian, sculpture by Cyrus Dallin can be found in the park between the Arlington Library and Arlington Town Hall on Massachusetts Avenue.

European descent.

The Christian Nipmuc of central Massachusetts were similarly reduced in numbers by earlier wars in the 18th century that left women and children in difficult straits. Like the Mashpees, the Hassanamisco Nipmuc in Grafton had been assigned white guardians who went off to fight in the Revolutionary War, but their replacements were incompetent, further reducing the circumstances of Nipmuc families. Forbears of the Cisco family, that has produced leaders in this century, had to sell most of their land at that time to survive. The Nipmuc, who were not getting along well with their white neighbors, tended to be Loyalists.

More impacted were the descendants of Natick, a "praying town" west of Boston, one of the communities of Christian Indians founded by Minister John Eliot. Following the Revolution, Natick had lost all its males, leaving only widows and children.

Crispus Attucks, the first man to die in the Boston Massacre in 1770, was of mixed African and Native ancestry, and had a Natick father. The name "Attucks" is Algonquian for "deer."

The Natick and Nipmuc communities had at an earlier time absorbed the Christian Indian village of Nashoba (located in what is now Littleton). Nashoba villagers were originally inhabitants of the Concord area, which Indians then called "Musketaquid." Previously Musketaquid's Natives had been displaced by the very English settlers, who bought their land in Musketaquid. The new settlers were led by fur trader Simon Willard from Kent and by John Jones and Peter Bulkeley, two ministers who had been forbidden to preach in England because of their divergent religious beliefs. In 1635 they received a charter from the Massachusetts General Court (legislature) to found a village, modeled after those they had left behind in England. Their new town was to be called "Concord," supposedly to reflect the agreement and harmony between the new British settlers and the former Native inhabitants. Ironically, there was to be no future harmony between the new settlers and the Natives, because the settlers' plans for their new village did not include any future continued settlement by its original Natives. Musketaquid's Natives were completely displaced by these new settlers and they were forced to move from Concord, north to Nashoba.

During King Philip's War in the 1670s, the converted Christian "praying Indians" of Nashoba fought on the side of the English against their unconverted Native brothers and sisters. Soon Christian Indians were removed to Concord (from whence they had come) by their colonist "protectors," presumably for their safety. However, betrayed by Concord's fearful citizens, these Christian Indians were exiled to Deer Island in the Boston Harbor, leaving only twelve men there to protect 46 women and children. Only fifty of the original 58 returned; presumably' eight died of starvation or were sold as slaves. The survivors eventually returned from their captivity, but stayed only briefly at Nashoba. Most then moved to Natick to live among the Nipmuc (Gookin).

While in Concord, the Nashoba Indians were taught by a Christian Nipmuc woman. The woman's husband, Joseph, had been a trusted guide to the English, but due to a "want of shelter, protection and encouragement," he eventually changed sides. Captured by the British with his two children in Plymouth, the three were sold as slaves to a Boston merchant, who promptly shipped Joseph to Jamaica to work as a slave. At that point, the minister John Elliot intervened and purchased the two children, then returned them to their mother. He also insisted that Joseph be brought back. Joseph was returned, but remained a domestic slave in Boston (Gookin).

Despite the loss of men, women, land, and possessions in the centuries following European arrival and long after the American Revolution, the Algonquian peoples of Massachusetts have shown adaptability and persistence, and in this century have felt able once again to claim their identity openly. Today on any summer weekend a visitor may find a pow-wow (dance celebration) in progress in some Massachusetts town, and is welcome to participate in the revival of American Indian culture and society that is being taking place across America.

★ NATIVE AMERICANS ★

Algonquian Place Names That Live Today

★ **Massachusetts**—Our state is named for the Massachusett tribe of coastal Algonquians. The state seal has always included a Native American.

★ **Musketaquid**–grassy, reedy river (Native name for today's Concord).

★ **Menotomy**–swift running waters, the name Algonquians and, later, early English settlers gave to their village between Cambridge and Lexington – today's Arlington.

★ **Annursnac**–the summit or lookout; one of Concord's three large hills, retains its original Algonquian name.

★ **Nashawtuc**–between two rivers; Nashawtuc Hill in Concord is between the Assabet and Sudbury Rivers before they converge to form the Concord River.

★ **Punkatasset**–shallow brook hill. It was to Punkatasset Hill that Concord's militia and Minutemen gathered after their strategic withdrawal from Concord village, as Col. Smith's 700 plus British Regulars marched into Concord from Lexington early on the morning of April 19, 1775. The Americans regrouped and grew in strength, when soldiers from many other neighboring towns joined them there, before they descended to the North Bridge to face the British and fire "the shot heard round the world."

★ **Assabet**– a swampy place. The Assabet River starts in the town of Westborough and winds 32 miles through primal woodlands as well as past mill cities before joining the Sudbury River to form the Concord River. Egg Rock, where the two rivers merge, was a gathering spot for Native Americans for thousands of years. All three rivers are popular with canoeists and kayakers today.

★ **Squaw Sachem Trail** in Concord is named for the woman (squaw) who served as Sachem (leader) of the Algonqian Natives, who in 1635 negotiated sale of "six myles square" of their land at Musketaquid to British settlers, and who renamed the new town Concord.

Sources:

Blancke, Shirley and Barbara Robinson. *From Musketaquid to Concord: The Native and European Experience. Concord Museum, Concord, MA, 1985.*

Calloway, Colin G.,*The American Revolution in Indian Country. Cambridge University Press, 1995.*

Campisi, Jack, *The Mashpee Indians: Tribe on Trial. Syracuse University Press, 1991.*

Gookin, Daniel, *An Historical Account of the Doings and Sufferings of the Christian Indians in New England in the years 1675-7, 1677.*

Gardner, Russell (Great Moose), *Personal communication from Gardner, Wampanoag tribal historian, about a document discovered by Jeremy Bangs, formerly visiting curator of Pilgrim Hall in Plymouth.*

Huden, John C., *Indian Place Names in New England, Heye Foundation, New York, 1962*

Mandell, Daniel R.Behind the Frontier: Indians in Eighteenth-Century Eastern Massachusetts. University of Nebraska Press, 1996.*

MUSTER ROLL OF MASSACHUSETTS TOWNS WHO SENT MILITIA AND/OR MINUTE MEN TO THE BATTLE OF APRIL 19, 1775

ACTON
Davis's Company
Hunt's Company
Robin's Company

ARLINGTON
Locke's Company

BEDFORD
Moore's Company
Willson's Company

BEVERLY
Dodge's Company
Thorndike's Company
Shaw's Company

BILLERICA
Crosby's Company
Farmer's Company
Stickney's Company

BROOKLINE
White's Company
Aspinwall's Company
Gardner's Company

CAMBRIDGE
Locke's Company
Thatcher's Company

CHELMSFORD
Barron's Company
Parkers' Company

CONCORD
Brown's Company
Mile's Company
Minot's Company
Barrett's Company

DANVERS
Epes's Company
Flint's Company
Hutchinson's Company

Lowe's Company
Page's Company
Prince's Company
Edmund Putnam's Co.
John Putnam's Co.

DEDHAM
Battle's Company
Bullard's Company
Draper's Company
Ellis's Company
Fairbank's Company
Fuller's Company
Gould's Company
Guild's Company

DRACUT
Coburn's Company
Russell's Company

FRAMINGHAM
Edget's Company
Emen's Company
Gleason's Company

LEXINGTON
Parker's Company

LINCOLN
Smith's Company
Stone's Company

LYNN
Bancroft's Company
Farrington's Company
Mansfield's Company
Newhall's Company
Parker's Company

MALDEN
Blaney's Company

MEDFORD
Hall's Company

NEEDHAM
Aaron Smith's Company
Robert Smith's Company
Kingsbery's Company

NEWTON
Cook's or Marean's Co.
Fuller's Company
Wiswall's Company

READING
Bacheller's Company
Eatons's Company
Flint's Company
Walton's Company

ROXBURY
Child's Company
Draper's Company
Whiting's Company

STOW
Whitcom's Company

SUDBURY
Cudworth's Company
Haynes's Company
Locker's Company
Nixon's Company
Smith's Company
Stone's Company

WATERTOWN
Bate's Company

WESTFORD
Minot's Company
Parker's Company

WOBURN
Belknap's Company
Fox's Company
Walker's Company

Source: Coburn, Frank Warren. Muster Rolls of the Participating Companies of American Militia and Minutemen in the Battle of April 19, 1775. Eastern National Parks & Monument Association, 1995.

★ ★ ★ ★

Colonial Idioms Alive Today

BY D. MICHAEL RYAN

★ **"Flash in the pan."**
★ **"At loggerheads."**
★ **"Read the riot act."**
★ **"A wind fall."**

Colorful idioms all, and what they share in common is a modern usage connected to an 18th Century past. While today's meaning may differ, these terms and others might have been heard around Concord Town in 1775. Come listen and discover the fascinating origins of some peculiar phrases.

When colonial gunsmith Joshia Meriam constructed a musket, it was usually accomplished and paid for in three parts—lock (firing

"Flash in the pan" refers to musket powder exploding without firing a musket ball, that is a misfire.

mechanism), stock (wood), and barrel (metal tube). Once completed the item as a whole was given to its owner. Today when one obtains an item with all its parts, it is owned **"lock, stock and barrel."** If militia man Thaddeus Blood placed his musket in the safety position (half-cocked) then he entered battle, he had better remember to advance to full-cock or the weapon would not fire and he would be in trouble. A person **"going off half-cocked"** is not successful due to lack of preparation and forethought.

Nathan Stowe might prime his musket (small measure of powder in the pan), load the main charge to the barrel, fire, only to have the priming powder explode. This was known as a **"flash in the pan"** or misfire. Today, the term means a sudden brief success not likely to be repeated or followed by a greater success. Stowe might need a new flint, but being unable to afford or unwilling to pay for such, he will take a knife and chip or skin pieces from the old flint until it is serviceable. Today, a cheap or thrifty person is called **"a skin flint."**

Other idioms may be traced to 18th Century taverns. Thomas Munroe, tavern keep, might use chalk to mark upon his wall the bill of a patron who wished to pay

THE MINUTE MAN N.H.P.

at a later time. this was a reminder to collect owed money. Something is **"chalked up"** to experience in our world, meaning that, while unfortunate, it is not regretted by an attempt will be made to insure it does not happen again. An account mark is made in the memory. Today, people who quarrel or enter a confrontation are said to be **"at logger Heads."** Colonial tavern keep Amos Wright used a heated loggerhead (long metal bar with a ball on the end) to warm drinks. Patrons sometimes used them in fights.

Grog was a cheap 18th Century drink of rum and water invented by a ship's captain to water down sailor's daily liquor ration in hopes of ending drunken brawls. Today one who consumes too much spirits may appear **"groggy"** or mildly intoxicated. Keeper Ephraim Jones might yell to rowdy patrons to **"mind their p's and q's"** (pints and quarts of drink) and today the term still refers to watching ones manners and conduct; behaving properly. Today, a **"rule of thumb"** is a way to accomplish a task based on experience rather than theory or careful calculation. A colonial brewer (without a thermometer) would dip his thumb into a mixture to determine when the liquid was the right temperature to add the yeast.

If we receive unexpected good fortune (usually money) it is called **"a wind fall."** For Jonas Bateman in the 1770's it meant that trees or limbs were blown down and easily obtained for firewood. Also, the King's agents marked certain trees for use by the Royal Navy. Tampering with them resulted in severe punishment. If a storm blew the tree down, it could be claimed by anyone—a wind fall.

Have you ever been **"read the riot act"** or informed in an angry manner that your conduct was wrong and must stop? The Riot Act of 1715 was meant to address groups gathering and threatening the peace. A magistrate could read part of the Act, commanding people to disperse in the King's name or face action. In the 1880's Americans began using the term to mean "scold."

Purchase Brown, 1770's farmer, would **"ear mark"** his animals with a distinctive brand to denote ownership or purpose. Citizens would gather annually on muster day to watch the militia drill, enjoy food and drink, socialize and have a fun time. They had a **"field day."** When John Buttrick, Jr. retired for the night, he probably would sleep on bedding of straw and thus in today's usage he would **"hit the hay."** Meliscent Barrett might have the rope supports between the wooden sides of her bed frame tightened (no metal springs) to insure a good night's sleep. As today, she would be requested to **"sleep tight."**

When next you hear a modern idiom, ask if it has origins in the 18th Century and might have been used in 1775 Concord. In selecting to read this article, you took **"pot luck"** — what was available, not for sure what you might receive. Had you visited my home or tavern 225 years ago and I had not had the chance to prepare a proper meal, you would have eaten whatever was in the oven pot... taken a chance... taken pot luck.

Sources:
Kirkpatrick, E.M. and Schwarz, C.M., The Wordsworth Dictionary of Idioms, 1995;
Ledered, Richard M. Jr., Colonial American English, 1985.

★ ★ ★ ★

About the Author

Joseph Lyon "Joel" Andrews, Jr., M.D. is a physician, author, social and environmental activist and history buff. A resident of Concord, Masssachusetts and a former resident of Boston, Dr. Andrews is a Licensed Concord Guide, Founder and Director of the Concord Guides Walking Tours, an associate member of the Concord Historical Commission and a representative to the Lexington-Concord Area Visitors Association.

His own family's Revolutionary heritage helped to spark the curiosity that led to his researching and writing this book. He is a descendent of Revolutionary War soldiers and Patriots, including Haym Salomon, often called "Financier of the Revolution." Dr. Andrews serves as Surgeon of the Massachusetts Society of the Sons of the American Revolution (S.A.R.). He is a free-lance writer and photographer for *The Boston Globe* and other publications. He writes about history, medicine, travel, as well as about environmental, social, cultural, religious and human rights issues.

Born in Manhattan, he grew up in Georgetown, D.C. and Scarsdale, N.Y. He graduated from Amherst College and the U. of Rochester School of Medicine and trained in internal medicine at the Boston City Hospital and in pulmonary medicine at Massachusetts General Hospital. Dr. Andrews served as a Captain in the U.S Air Force Medical Corps in the Pacific during the Viet Nam era. He has studied, worked, practiced and taught medicine in many countries, including Argentina, England, Sweden, Russia, India, Thailand, Japan, Australia, Spain, Kenya, France, Belgium, Germany and Israel.

Dr. Andrews is a practicing internist/pulmonologist and Lecturer in Medicine at Tufts University School of Medicine.

★ ★ ★ ★

About the Contributors

★ **Shirley Blancke** is Associate Curator of Archeology and Native American Studies at the Concord Museum. Originally from London, she studied anthropology and archeology at Cambridge and Boston Universities. She resides in Concord.

★ **Jay Cannon** is a Sudbury Minuteman and a life-long Revolutionary history buff and Colonial re-enactor and former publisher of *Yankee Doodle*, a magazine for Revolutionary re-enactors. He lives in Concord with his family.

★ **Elizabeth "Betsy" Conant** is a long time resident of Acton and active member of the Acton Historical Society, for which she helped edit *A Brief History of Acton* for the Bicentennial.

★ **John Filios** of Bedford is a member of the Bedford Minutemen, where he pursues his interest in local Revolutionary history. He retired as a Lieutenant Colonel from the U. S. Air Force.

★ **Donald L. Hafner** is a Captain in the Lincoln Minutemen. He is a Professor of Political Science at Boston College and resides in Belmont.

★ **D. Michael Ryan** of Concord is Historian of the Concord Minutemen, and an 18th Century Volunteer Interpreter with the National Park Service. He is Associate Dean of Students at Boston College. A native of Gloucester, he served as an Army Ranger in Vietnam.

★ **Lou Sideris** is Chief of Interpretations at Minutemen National Historical Park Lexington and Concord, MA. A graduate of the University of California, he has worked for the National Park Service at Sequoia and Yellowstone Parks and has been at Minuteman Park for over ten years. His most recent assignment was as advisor to Nepal's Park Service in the Himalayas.

★ **David Stonecliff** was Co-editor of the Acton Historical Society's *A Brief History of Acton in 1976*, from which our Acton Chapter is adopted. He now resides in Florida.

★ ★ ★ ★

Acknowledgements

ublication of this book was truly a collaborate effort. I am very thankful to the outside authors, who, contributed individual chapters about areas of their expertise. I deeply appreciate the work and enthusiasm of these authors: Shirley Blancke, Jay Cannon, Betsy Conant, John Filios, Donald L. Hafner, D. Michael Ryan, Lou Sideris, and David Stonecliffe.

I am indebted particularly to my children, Jennifer, Sara and Joe, who contributed in so many ways, from research to editing to writing to photo scanning to marketing. This was really a family project. I am grateful for the editorial review by my sisters, Lynn Andrews Kotzen and Dale Andrews Eldridge and by my niece, Debbie Kotzen, and for the computer assistance of my nephew, Daniel Eldridge, who designed our spiffy Web site for Concord Guides & Press. I am indebted to Jane Luna Rieger for her careful review of the manuscript and for her suggestions for improving it and to Darlene Bisceglia for her help in many areas.

I owe special thanks to Valerie Bessette, whose skills as a graphic designer and whose diligent work has added immeasurably to the coherence, as well as the appearance, of this book. I am also grateful to the over 80 Sponsors whose support of this project has made possible the publication and distribution of this book and its sale at a reasonable price.

I give my heartfelt thanks to many other people and organizations, whose assistance was crucial in producing this book. Win Williams, Editor of the *S.A.R. Magazine*, did a wonderful job at editing and formatting the article (Spring, 1997), that eventually served as the basis for this book. The staff at Minute Man Press in West Concord worked incredibly long hours to publish the First Edition; my hat goes off to Jim and Kathy Steinmann and Karen Rogers. Jim Coveno of Data Associates, and Ted Demetriades and his staff at Inter City Press in Rockland, MA. are responsible for the quality printing of the Second Edition. Typists Wendy Sullivan, Brenda Savoy, Edie Cretec, Maura Haberman and Linda Anderson provided invaluable assistance.

Careful review of the text, along with constructive criticism, was done by Jane Alexander, D. Michael Ryan and members of the Book Club of the Concord-Carlisle Newcomers' Club, as well as many friends and members of my family. Frequent helpful advice about the most appropriate content and style for the book has been given to me by Dale Szeceblowski and Christie Johnson of the Concord Bookstore, by Valerie Cariagianes and Jim Hayden of Eastern National and by Charles Bahne, author of *The Complete Guide to Boston's Freedom Trail.* Eminent history professors at Brandeis University, David H. Fischer and Jonathan Sarna, have been very kind in giving me the benefit of their extensive historical knowledge and perspectives in reviewing material for this book.

National Park Service staff members who have been particularly helpful in many

★ ACKNOWLEDGEMENTS ★

areas are: at Minute Man National Historic Park, Nancy Nelson (Superintendent), Lou Sideris (Chief of Interpretation), Douglas Sabin (Historian), Mark Nichapor and Clint Jackson; at Longfellow House in Cambridge, Kelley Fellner; and at Bunker Hill, Doug Gagnon, Ranger. I am thankful to many compatriots of the Sons of the American Revolution (S.A.R.) at both the state and national levels for their help and support.

In Concord I am indebted to historians Tom Blanding Judy Crockett, Jayne Gordon and Tedd Osgood, as well as to my fellow Concord Guides and to fellow members of the Concord Historical Commission, Concord Historical Collaborative, the Lexington-Concord Area Visitors Association, the Concord Chamber of Commerce, the Concord Museum, Orchard House, the Old Manse and the Concord Free Public Library, particularly Marcia Moss and Leslie Wilson of Special Collections, Barbara Powell (Director) and Ray Gerke. In Lexington I have been helped by Christine Ellis, George Comptois and Skip Haywood of the Lexington Historical Society, the late Thomas Leavitt (Director) and John Hamilton (Curator) from the Museum of Our National Heritage and Marcy Quill, Director of the Lexington Chamber of Commerce.

Special thanks too go to many individuals, who were generous with their time in serving as resources for their towns' unique Revolutionary histories: in Acton, Earle Nadeau of the Acton Minutemen and Betsy Conant from the Acton Historical Society; in Arlington, Lisa Welter of the Arlington Historical Society; in Bedford, Sharon McDonald from the Bedford Library. In Cambridge I was helped by Aurore Eaton of the Cambridge Historical Society and Kit Rollins from the Cambridge Historical Commission; and in Sudbury by Carol Coutrier, and by Guy LaBlanc and Richard Gnatowski of the Wayside Inn and by Lee Swanson from the Sudbury Historical Society. In Boston I received assistance from Jennifer Tolpa at the Massachusetts Historical Society, Sara Leaf-Herman at the Freedom Trail Foundation, Patrick Leahy, Research Coordinator at the Paul Revere House and Renee Meyer, Manager of the Boston Tea Party Ship and Museum.

I am grateful to Katie Ohara, Kit Jurrens and to Marcus Maronn for their help in receiving support from our more than 80 Sponsors, whose backing was so important for making this book a reality.

★ Guide to Sponsors ★

Much of the written material in this book was first published in an article by Joseph L. Andrews, M.D., (Lexington & Concord: 1775 / 1997) in the Sons of the American Revolution (S.A.R.) Magazine Spring 1997, and is reprinted here with the kind permission of the National Society Sons of the American Revolution.

The Sons of the American Revolution is a national and international organization of over 26,000 male descendants of soldiers and patriots who supported the American struggle for independence during the American Revolution (1775 / 1783). New members are welcome. Inquiries can be made by mail to:

NASSAR
1000 South Fourth Street
Louisville, KY 40203

or by telephone at (502) 589 - 1776, or to local and state S.A.R. societies.

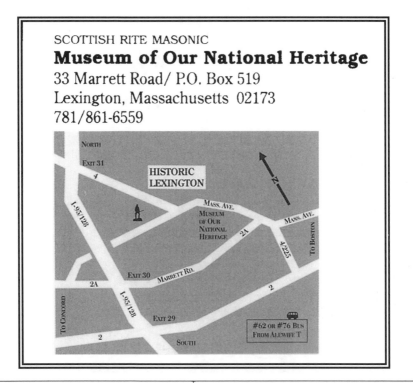

THE WESTIN
WALTHAM-BOSTON

TEL: 781-290-5607
HOTEL: 781-290-5600
FAX: 781-890-7576

70 Third Avenue
Waltham, MA 02451-7523

Sheraton Lexington
Inn

727 Marrett Road, Lexington, Massachusetts 02421
Tel: (781) 862-8700, ext. 323 • FAX: (781) 861-9642

★ LODGING ★

★ RESTAURANTS ★

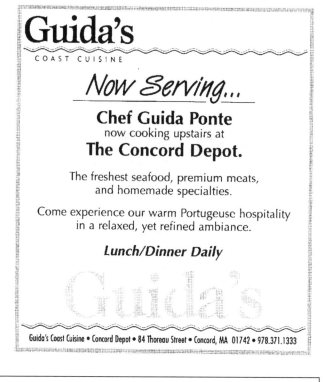

★ FURNITURE, ANTIQUES & GIFT SHOPS ★

Antiques   *Accessories*

North Bridge Antiques

Tuttle's Livery
45 Walden Street

Concord, MA 01742
(978) 371-1442

★ GIFT SHOPS ★

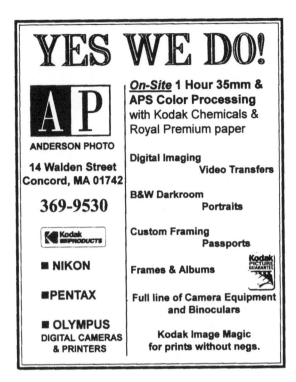

★ SPECIALTY SHOPS ★

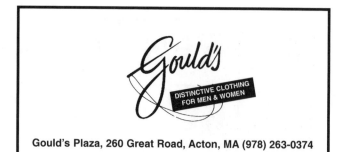

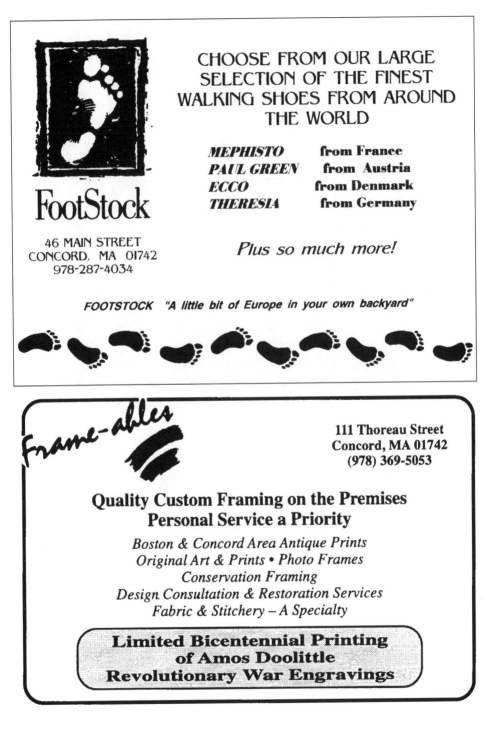

THE REALTY GUILD, INC.

1998 Sales Volume Achievement Award
$13 MILLION AND MORE

Personalized, Attentive, Superior Service

from

Susan Revis

Certified Residential Specialist

of

J.M. Barrett & Co., Inc.

Walden Street, Concord

978 369 6453

Concord Shoe Repair

100 Commonwealth Avenue
Concord, MA 01742

ARNOLD & KANGAS, P. C.

Counsellors at Law

Damonmill Square, Suite 5D
9 Pond Lane
Concord, MA 01742-2842

Jeanne S. Kangas

Telephone 978.369.0001
Facsimile 978.371.2378
E-Mail AK0001@aol.com

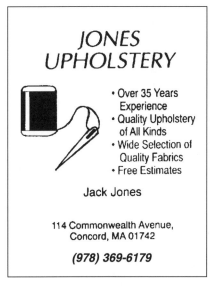

JONES UPHOLSTERY

- Over 35 Years Experience
- Quality Upholstery of All Kinds
- Wide Selection of Quality Fabrics
- Free Estimates

Jack Jones

114 Commonwealth Avenue,
Concord, MA 01742

(978) 369-6179

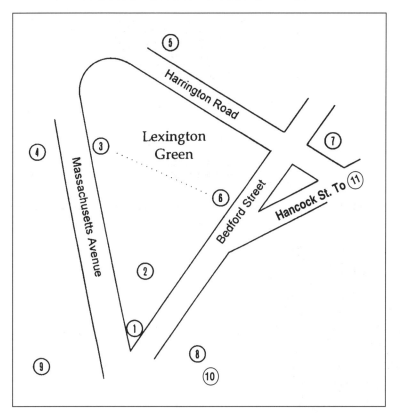

This map highlights some sites important in Lexington's history. Start your walk at the Minuteman Statue and enjoy your visit.

1. The Lexington Minuteman Statue (1900)
2. The Flag
3. The Revolutionary War Monument (1799)
4. Hancock United Church of Christ (1868)
5. First Parish Church (1692, 1847)
6. Parker Boulder (1775)
7. Masonic Temple (1839)
8. Buckman Tavern (1710)
9. The Belfry (1761)
10. Lexington Visitors' Center
11. Hancock-Clark House (1698)

Courtesy of the Lexington Historical Society

★ MAP OF CONCORD ★

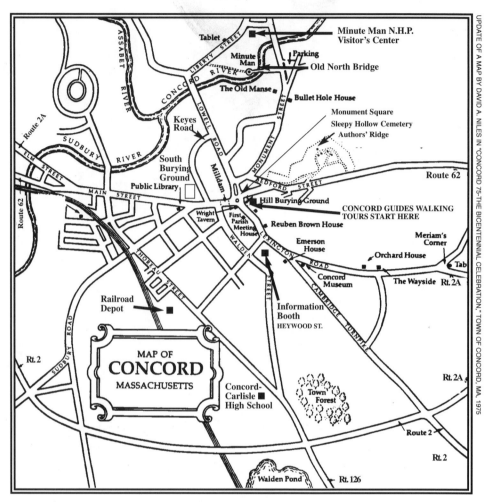

UPDATE OF A MAP BY DAVID A. NILES IN "CONCORD 75-THE BICENTENNIAL CELEBRATION." TOWN OF CONCORD, MA, 1975

Back Cover Photograph–North Bridge, Concord, MA

Spanning the Concord River - "the rude bridge that arched the flood" (Emerson) Concord's North Bridge on April 19, 1775 was the scene of the first American resistance to the armed might of the British Empire. The American Patriot farmer - soldiers returned musket fire against the British Regulars, killing three of them. Two Americans were killed. The American Revolution had begun! (Photo courtesy of Minute Man National Historical Park) shows Colonial Militia historic interpreters marching on Patriots' Day.